DIY BEER BREWING

DO-IT-YOURSELF BREWING

Is the art of beer brewing new to you?
Dive right in and whip up a batch in no time.

- Assemble your beer kit: You'll need equipment from brewing through bottling

- Decide your recipe and seek out the freshest ingredients

- Plan your brew day: Making beer is a timely process; avoid disruption on brew days

- Monitor your fermentation, including location and temperature controls

- Learn more about making beer from online and local homebrew groups

Happy Beer Brewing!

ASTRID COOK

DIY BEER BREWING

CREATING YOUR FIRST HOMEBREW

ROCKRIDGE
PRESS

For general information on our other products and services or to obtain technical support, please contact our Customer Care Department within the United States at (866) 744-2665, or outside the United States at (510) 253-0500.

Rockridge Press publishes its books in a variety of electronic and print formats. Some content that appears in print may not be available in electronic books, and vice versa.

TRADEMARKS: Rockridge Press and the Rockridge Press logo are trademarks or registered trademarks of Callisto Media Inc. and/or its affiliates, in the United States and other countries, and may not be used without written permission. All other trademarks are the property of their respective owners. Rockridge Press is not associated with any product or vendor mentioned in this book.

Front and back cover photography © Suzanne Clements; Interior photography © Suzanne Clements p. 2, 3, 6, 8, 16, 22, 36, 58, 76, 84; StockFood/Joff Lee, p. 53; Stocksy/Kirsty Begg p. 66; StockFood/Bodo A. Schieren, p. 79

Illustrations © 2015 by Tom Bingham

ISBN: Print 978-1-62315-670-1 | eBook 978-1-62315-682-4

CONTENTS

INTRODUCTION

There are three brews that beer drinkers always recall: the very first beer they tried (probably an illicit childhood sip), the first truly remarkable beer they drank (perhaps a venerable European import) and the first beer they brewed themselves.

If you've never brewed beer for yourself, you're missing out on one of the three best beer memories you could ever have. This book is for beer lovers who are ready to make the foray into beer brewing with minimal effort, hoping to spend as little money and time as possible to create tasty homebrewed beer. It's also for DIY (do it yourself) brewers with only a layperson's knowledge who feel that the history, style variations, and full brewing setup can wait until after their glorious first homebrewing experience. This book puts you in the express lane, providing the exact amount of information you need to become smart, knowledgeable, and savvy about beer brewing—fast.

Nearly every major craft brewery in the United States was launched by someone who began as a homebrewer. Many of them are winning gold medals at national beer festivals, gaining fans, and selling their beers in local pubs and retail shops. The future is wide open for a homebrewer with a great beer.

For anyone who grew up drinking mass-produced lager (e.g., Budweiser or Coors), the variety of beer you can make at home might come as a surprise. The growing diversity of beer styles over the last generation or so might be a revelation to you. The time and effort beer experts have put into defining beer styles is considerable, giving homebrewers a clear set of guidelines as to how each type of beer should look and, of course, taste. Plus, brewing beer is fun. Creating beer that tastes just right for your palate has never been easier, with homebrew clubs and DIY shops popping up all over the country and online.

What are you waiting for? Let's brew some beer!

1

DIVE RIGHT IN

You don't have to have a degree in brewing science to make good beer. In fact, you can dive right in to brewing once you've assembled the ingredients and equipment you'll need to brew at home. After you've tasted the good beer you've brewed yourself, you'll want to try more complicated recipes and learn more about how to make great beers.

You'll begin brewing with an easy beer recipe whose simple instructions guide you through your first beer-making experience. By substituting *liquid malt extract* (terms in *italics* are defined in the Glossary) for *all-grain mash*, this homebrew recipe will give you a 24-bottle case of amber *ale* that will be fully finished in about a month (you can start sampling it in a mere two weeks).

As American Homebrewers Association (AHA) founder Charlie Papazian famously noted, homebrewing should be a relaxing activity. So, try not to worry, and get ready to join the millions of others who have blazed the trail for you.

EASY AS 1, 2, 3, . . . 10!

There are 10 basic steps to brewing beer:

1. Clean and sanitize your brewing equipment and tools.

2. Create the mash from *malted barley* or another grain (this step is skipped in *all-extract* brewing, the process you'll learn in this chapter).

3. Filter out grains from your liquid *wort* (pronounced "wert"), a process also known as *lautering* (skipped in all-extract brewing).

4. Boil the wort.

5. Add *hops*, sugar, and additional (optional) ingredients.

6. Cool and oxygenate the wort.

7. *Pitch* the *yeast*.

8. Ferment your beer.

9. Bottle your beer.

10. Drink your beer.

That's it! Ten steps (for this first recipe, reduced to eight) to make your debut batch of homebrew. Although there are an infinite number of recipes for beer, you'll start off with a basic, surefire recipe for amber ale made with liquid malt extract. After about two hours of preparation, you'll know the fundamentals of how to make beer, and within a couple of weeks you'll have a good, drinkable beer as a reward for your efforts.

The steps of brewing are the same for all beers. Yes, even the big shots at Anheuser-Busch use these steps to make their beer on a massive scale. However, most homebrewers work with no more than 5 gallons of beer at a time. In fact, you can make beer in very manageable 1-gallon batches: Many recipe kits come in this size. The recipes in this book should net you 2½ gallons of beer—roughly one case of 24 12-ounce bottles.

There are no hard-and-fast measurements or ingredients in brewing, but some brewers are quite specific as to the procedure they use. The truth is that making beer predates thermometers, timers, and notions of food contamination. In fact, brewing even predates the use of hops, which today are considered one of the four key beer ingredients—alongside water, malt, and yeast—and have only been a part of beer recipes for a few hundred years. Even if your wort gets contaminated during the brew process, barring any major problem (e.g., your cat decides to float its toys in your *brew pot*), allow nature to do what it does best: create your beer. Throwing away perfectly drinkable beer, even a batch with *off-flavors*, isn't just a waste of beer but a loss of key information. You'll learn as much from your mistakes as you will your successes. Plus, when you gain the confidence to experiment with your own recipes, you'll be making "mistakes of fortune" that so many great brewers have also made in their efforts to create new styles of beer. In other words, try your best and, invariably, you'll succeed in making beer.

A caveat: Although you can start brewing immediately without a lot of "do this first" distractions, you'll need to gather some basic brewing equipment (see chapter 3 for an equipment list). Be sure to look at the optional equipment as well, so you don't get to the middle of a recipe (even a quick-start recipe such as the one in this chapter) only to find you're one can opener shy of your homebrew. Leaving your brew to rush out for more gear or ingredients won't ruin your beer, but it may disrupt your timing (yeast don't grow on trees . . . oh, wait . . .). If you have to go back online or out to your brew shop for an ingredient or equipment you don't have, you'll have to postpone your brew day and your homebrew revelry, and you may even scuttle your first batch. Especially if you're employing an "enjoy beer as you brew" methodology, you should have everything set out and ready to go (particularly the yeast; you cannot make beer without yeast). A few minutes of preparation time will save you the grief of losing your batch to poor planning.

DID YOU KNOW?

If you can cook, you can make beer. There are plenty of beer recipes that are no more difficult than boiling pasta in water! So long as you don't burn your batch, you'll brew up good, truly drinkable beer.

BREW THE PERFECT BATCH

To ensure that your first batch of homebrew is perfect, use only the freshest ingredients. The New Brew Amber Ale recipe uses malt extracts, which degrade when oxidized (i.e., when exposed to air). Look for expiration dates and problems with packaging, such as dents in cans or tears in bags. If you're shopping for supplies online, check independent sources, such as homebrewing forums, for reviews of the product the retailer is selling. If you're shopping at a homebrew supply store in person, ask the staff and other customers questions to make sure you're dealing with knowledgeable beer makers.

Whether your inaugural beer is the best you've ever tasted or seriously lacking in some way, you'll only be able to replicate or correct it the next time if you carefully document your experience. As you brew, keep track of your activity and any unusual events (e.g., boil-overs, accidentally using a non-sanitized spoon). When you finally get to drink this batch in a few weeks, you won't remember everything you did during the cooking process, so proper note taking is essential for your "beerduction."

There are a lot of variables to consider and choices to make in homebrewing, but for now, simply follow the recipe directions so you can make your first beer without having to figure out why you're doing what you're doing. Afterward, while you wait out the fermentation process, you can read more of this book to learn about the hows and whys of brewing.

STEP-BY-STEP PROCESS FOR FIRST-TIME HOMEBREWERS

4. STEEP YOUR GRAINS (FOR ALL-GRAIN BATCHES)

Most brewers prefer to use a mesh bag to steep grains, but you can use a sanitized stainless steel strainer as well.

1. BUY YOUR EQUIPMENT

The first step is to put together a kit. For first time homebrewers, it's recommended to consult a brick-and-mortar shop rather than buying online (if cost is prohibitive, check with homebrew clubs in the area and buy a used set-up). Don't forget to buy sanitizer and cleaning equipment.

2. BUY YOUR INGREDIENTS

Fresh is best. At a minimum, you'll be purchasing malt (either in grains or extract format or both), hops (in cone or pellet form or both), yeast (dry or liquid) and priming sugar.

3. SANITIZE THE EQUIPMENT

Cleanliness is the key to beer free of off-flavors.

5. RINSE—I.E. SPARGE—YOUR GRAINS (FOR ALL-GRAIN BATCHES)

To get all the sugars from your spent grain, either pour hot water over your draining mesh bag or through the grain strained via above-mentioned strainer.

6. ADD LIQUID MALT EXTRACT (IF USING) TO PRE-BOILED AND REHEATED WATER

If you are using LME rather than all-grain, skip steps 4 and 5 and add the malt extract to clean (pre-boiled or filtered) water when water is hot but pre-boiling. If you are using LME in addition to grains, add the malt extract directly into the pre-boiling wort.

7. BOIL THE WORT

Most recipes require the wort to boil for an hour; be sure to watch for the first hard break to avoid a huge mess on your stove (not to mention the loss of precious wort).

8. ADD HOPS (AS NECESSARY) AND/OR IRISH MOSS

Hops (in any form) can be added at various points during the boil depending on the recipe; Irish Moss is typically added post-boil to reduce protein build-up in the wort.

9. REMOVE ANY MESH BAGS AND DETRITUS AT END OF BOIL; COVER THE BOILING POT

Wort should be clear of ingredients prior to chilling. If you brew in a bag, simply remove the entire mesh lining and only wort will remain in your boiling pot.

10. CHILL THE WORT

Whether using an ice bath or a wort chiller, cool your wort as quickly as possible to avoid contaminants.

11. PREPARE YEAST (AS NECESSARY)

A good time to prepare dry yeast is while your wort is cooling; you may also warm (to room temperature) any liquid yeast or yeast starter that you will be using for your fermentation.

12. TRANSFER WORT TO SANITIZED FERMENTER (OR CARBOY, IF USING)

Simply pour from one container to the next, using a sanitized funnel if necessary.

13. ADD CLEAN (PRE-BOILED OR FILTERED) COOL WATER TO WORT IN SANITIZED FERMENTER

Top off your wort with the amount of water you need to make a full batch of beer.

14. MEASURE GRAVITY WITH A HYDROMETER (IF USING)

While this is optional, measuring original gravity will let you know how closely you came to making the exact beer style you set out to make and will allow you to determine alcohol content when the hydrometer is next used in your fermented beer.

15. PITCH THE YEAST

Simply add the prepared yeast to the wort (or from packet/vial in the case of liquid yeast).

16. PUT LID ON FERMENTER AND SHAKE TO AERATE THE WORT

For larger batches, you can pour the wort from the fermenter to a sanitized, food-grade bucket and back again.

17. ADD FERMENTER AIRLOCK; LEAVE TO FERMENT

Be sure to store your wort in a temperature-appropriate setting; this can be the back of a cool area for ales or a repurposed freezer for lagers. Be sure to monitor your fermenter for activity an optimal temperature. Expect a lot of activity the first couple of days.

18. RACK TO SECONDARY FERMENTER (IF USING)

If you want to eliminate trub and sediment—especially if you are going to dry hop or add additional ingredients such as fruits or coffee—rack to a secondary fermenter after a 2-3 days. By this point the fermentation should have slowed considerably, with bubbles percolating in the airlock approximately every 10 seconds.

19. RE-MEASURE GRAVITY WITH A HYDROMETER (IF USING)

Wait 2-4 weeks depending on recipe, and re-measure your gravity with a hydrometer to see if sufficient alcohol levels are present for your beer.

20. CREATE PRIMING SUGAR FOR BOTTLING

Once beer is ready to bottle, you will want to add sugar for carbonation.

21. ADD PRIMING SUGAR TO FERMENTER OR ADD TO BOTTLING BUCKET AND SIPHON FERMENTED BEER TO BOTTLING BUCKET

Mix the priming sugar with your beer. If you didn't rack to a secondary, you will want to siphon your beer to a second bucket with the priming sugar already in it. If your beer is already clean of trub (owing to a secondary fermentation), you can stir the sugar in gently prior to bottling.

22. TRANSFER BEER TO SANITIZED BOTTLES AND SEAL WITH SANITIZED CAPS

Be sure to fill bottles to the top, as the levels will decrease when you remove the bottling wand.

23. DRINK YOUR HOMEBREW!

HOMEBREWING EVENTS, ONLINE COMMUNITIES, AND WHERE TO BUY EQUIPMENT

EVENTS

American Homebrewers Association National Homebrewers Conference (ahaconference.org)—You'll undoubtedly have more fun and make more homebrewing friends at this conference than at any other homebrewing event you attend. Now in its 37th year, the conference attracts leading craft breweries, professional associations, homebrew clubs, retailers, beer educators, scientists, glass makers, and more.

Fresh Hop Ale Festival (freshhopalefestival.com)—This Yakima, Washington event is attended by more than 5,000 people and features a homebrew competition.

Great American Beer Festival (GABF) (greatamericanbeerfestival.com)—This is arguably the most popular beer festival in the world. Founded by the Brewers Association, the GABF is one of the oldest beer festivals in the United States and is attended by nearly 50,000 people every year. It's not a homebrewing festival per se, but it includes a ProAm competition in which professional brewers team up with homebrewers to create recipes that are judged in various categories.

Michigan Homebrew Festival (mhfsite.com)—This annual weekend in Michigan is largely attended by the Midwest homebrew community but is open to everyone. It offers people's choice awards.

ONLINE COMMUNITIES

American Homebrewers Association (homebrewersassociation.org)—Among its many resources is a search tool for finding a homebrew club near you.

The Brewing Network (thebrewingnetwork.com)—Here you'll find message boards, live chat, and a swag store that includes women's-cut homebrew T-shirts.

Home Brew Talk (homebrewtalk.com)—One of the best homebrew forums on the Internet, this site boasts a very active membership and a search tool for clubs.

WHERE TO BUY EQUIPMENT

American Homebrewers Association
(homebrewersassociation.org/lets-brew/
find-a-homebrew-supply-shop)—An excellent
site for finding recommendations for the best
places to buy equipment, the AHA also has a
homebrew supply shop search tool.

Austin Homebrew Supply
(austinhomebrew.com)—One of the most
popular online shops among homebrewers, this
retailer sells everything from the basics to grain
mills, chilling gear, and do-it-yourself parts. It
also offers cheese-making kits for whipping up
tasty cheeses to pair with your beer.

Bitter & Esters
(bitterandesters.com)—Located in Brooklyn,
New York, this retailer offers a full line of equipment and supplies, which are also available in
their online store. They also conduct homebrewing
classes. Best of all, for space-strapped homebrewers in New York City, the shop allows you to brew
on premises with its equipment, and provides
ingredients, advice from a master brewer, space
to leave the beer for fermentation, and tempera-
ture-controlled storage for bottle conditioning.

Craigslist
(craigslist.org)—You may be able to find full
equipment kits at a fraction of the cost of what
you'd pay in a store. All the normal Craigslist
caveats apply.

Keg Connection
(kegconnection.com)—This site sells homebrew
kits for kegging, as well as kegging supplies and
standard homebrew equipment.

Kegerator.com
(kegerator.com)—Here you can find high-end
refrigeration units and parts for building your
own *kegerator*.

William's Brewing
(williamsbrewing.com)—One of the oldest
homebrew suppliers in the United States,
William's sells whole equipment systems, keg
systems, and more.

NEW BREW AMBER ALE

MAKES ABOUT 2½ GALLONS

Sometimes called a red ale, this beer has a caramel flavor with a nice balance of hoppy bitterness and malty sweetness. The Willamette and Cascade hops used here are two of the many varieties of the bitter flower. Packaged brewing ingredients, including hops, are sold under numerous brand names, such as Muntons and Danstar. Before you set foot in your kitchen, assemble your tools (see chapter 3 for equipment descriptions).

5-gallon stainless steel or ceramic-coated steel stockpot (the brew pot)

1-quart glass jar

Food-grade liquid *sanitizer*

Floating or dial thermometer

Small saucepan

Large saucepan

Plastic wrap

Metal mesh strainer or 1–3 feet of food-grade plastic *siphon* tubing

3-gallon food-grade plastic bucket or plastic or glass *carboy*

Long-handled food-grade plastic spoon

Large food-grade funnel (if using a carboy)

Food-grade siphon hose (if using a bucket)

Airlock or *blowoff hose*

Digital room thermometer

1 (3.3-pound) can amber liquid malt extract (LME)

½ ounce dry Willamette hops (look for hops labeled "5% *alpha acid*")

½ ounce Cascade hops (look for hops labeled "5.5% alpha acid")

½ (11-gram/0.388-ounce) package Danstar Nottingham ale yeast (may substitute Fermentis Safale S-04 ale yeast)

1. In a 5-gallon brew pot over high heat, bring 2 gallons of water to a boil. Remove the brew pot from the heat. Transfer 2 cups of the water to a sanitized glass jar; set it aside to cool. Allow the water in the brew pot to cool to about 165°F.

2. Set the unopened can of LME in a small saucepan of hot, but not boiling, water for about 10 minutes to soften the contents to pouring consistency; do not overheat.

3. Pour the LME into the brew pot and stir gently until the LME dissolves completely and the water is evenly caramel-colored. The wort is now complete.

4. Return the brew pot to high heat and bring the wort to a boil. Watch for the *hot break*, when the wort will come close to boiling over. Reduce the heat so the wort doesn't boil over, but maintain a rolling boil.

5. Add the Willamette hops and boil for 60 minutes.

6. In a separate, clean saucepan, bring 1 gallon of water to a boil. Remove from the heat and allow the water to cool to room temperature. Set aside.

7. After 60 minutes of boiling the wort, remove it from the heat and add the Cascade hops. From this point on, make sure everything that comes into contact with the wort has been sanitized.

8. Carefully transfer the entire brew pot to a very icy bath (the kitchen sink, a bathtub, or a large cooler is good for holding an ice bath). Do not slow-chill the wort; it should take no longer than 30 minutes for the wort to cool to below 80°F.

9. Measure the temperature of the 2 cups of reserved boiled water. It should be between 95°F and 100°F. Do not add unsanitized water to cool or warm the reserved water; if necessary, reheat it or set it aside to cool further. Rehydrate the yeast by sprinkling it on top of the warm water and allowing it to dissolve. Loosely cover the jar with plastic wrap and set it aside for about 15 minutes, then gently swirl the solution.

10. Filter out the hops debris by pouring the chilled wort through a sanitized strainer into a sanitized 3-gallon food-grade bucket or carboy. Alternatively, stir the wort with a sanitized food-grade plastic spoon to bring the solid material to the center of the pot and use a sanitized siphon hose to draw the wort from the edge of the pot (this is called *whirlpooling*).

11. Add the boiled, cooled water from step 6 to the fermenting container to bring the total amount of wort to 2½ gallons. Shake the *fermenter* vigorously or pour the wort back and forth between the fermenter and brew pot to aerate it. Do not skip this process; the yeast need oxygen to reproduce, and shaking the wort adds air to the mix. Of course, don't shake so hard as to spill. Believe it or not, you now have beer. What you don't have is alcoholic beer.

12. Pitch (add) the yeast solution to the wort.

13. Cover the fermenter. The container should have an airlock with enough sanitizer in it so that no air can get into the fermenter. Alternatively, you can use a blowoff hose for the first couple of days (when vigorous fermentation can clog an airlock) and replace it with the airlock after the primary fermentation has taken place.

14. Now comes both the hardest and easiest part of the brewing process: Leave the fermenter alone. Yes, you'll worry and want to fuss over your "baby," but for the first 48 hours, trust that the yeast know what they're doing. You may notice a lot of activity in the airlock the first couple of days and nothing later. Remember Papazian's admonition: Don't worry. Just mind the fermentation temperature. The yeast used in this recipe works best between 58°F and 70°F. Simply attach a digital room thermometer to the outside of the fermenter to measure ambient temperature.

15. Wait 2 to 3 weeks. At this point the temperature should hold steady for three consecutive days. Your beer is drinkable now, but the standard fermentation process typically includes two more weeks for *bottle conditioning*.

BOTTLE YOUR BEER

After fermentation, there's one step left on the way from good beer to great beer: bottle conditioning. This is where handcrafted beer gets a lot of its bubbles compared with mass-produced commercial brands, which are carbonated like soda. It keeps fermenting in the sealed bottle, producing carbon dioxide that's got to go somewhere. As pressure builds up in the bottle, the gas dissolves in the beer. Open the bottle, and the carbonation comes bubbling out. Here's how to make the magic happen.

1. Assemble your tools (they're explained in Chapter 3): a brew pot or a *bottling bucket* with a spigot, 1–3 feet of food-grade plastic siphon tubing, 24 12-ounce beer bottles, 24 new bottle caps, a *bottle capper*, and food-grade liquid sanitizer. Sanitize the equipment according to the instructions in Chapter 3.

2. In a small saucepan over medium-high heat, boil 1/3 cup of *corn sugar* in 1 cup of water. Remove from the heat and cool the solution to 70°F.

3. Pour the sugar solution into the brew pot or bottling bucket.

4. Gently *rack* (transfer) the beer from the fermenting container to the bottling pot or bucket via sanitized siphon tubing. Try to keep the beer calm so the muck at the bottom (called *trub*, pronounced "troob" in the United States) doesn't get stirred up and mixed in. It's okay if a little of the sediment gets through, but stop racking when there's still about a half-inch of clear beer left on top of the trub.

5. Siphon 12 ounces of beer from the bottling container into a sanitized bottle, leaving a small air space at the top of the neck. (You may want to fill the bottles over a tray to catch spillage.) Cap each bottle immediately after filling it. This process is easier with two people, so that one of you can pour and the other can cap.

6. Let the bottles sit for another two weeks at 65°F to 75°F, away from sunlight. Bottles can (but shouldn't) blow their tops, so be sure to store them where they're not likely to cause injury or damage your property. An empty closet, spare bathroom, or cleared-out corner of your garage works well.

7. Taking care not to disturb any sediment at the bottom, gently place your finished bottles of beer in the refrigerator to chill.

8. Pop open a bottle and enjoy.

MASTER TIPS

The art of homebrewing can seem daunting if you think "the whole is greater than the sum of its parts." In fact, when it comes to gearing up, the opposite is true. To build your home brewery from scratch, you can purchase a reasonably priced beginner's 1-, 3-, or 5-gallon equipment kit from any decent homebrew supplier. The starter kit will probably sell for a substantial discount over a setup assembled from individual items. Either way, basic homebrewing equipment isn't expensive.

One of the reasons many beer lovers get into homebrewing is because it's affordable. You could spend a lot on a high-end, near-professional homebrew system (see chapter 3), but most homebrewers spend less than $100 to get started—and that includes ingredients for the first batch or two.

The recipes in this book, designed to make 2½ gallons of beer (i.e., 4 six-packs),

are manageable with a small setup, but you'll need additional or larger equipment if you want to move on to 5-gallon batches, the yield of most homebrew recipes. Once you start brewing standard 5-gallon batches, you'll need a larger brew pot that holds at least 8 (instead of 3) gallons, plus a 5-gallon fermenter. If you are looking to economize, you may want to buy a larger setup to start, knowing that a little more money spent now will mean less money spent later on.

Don't forget to join some online homebrew forums, where the buying and selling of equipment is common. There's always someone offering a setup kit at a discount, and you may want to sell your start-up system when you're ready to upgrade. Plus, online groups offer a lot of support and help when troubleshooting. Some of the best of these groups are listed on page 16.

2

OPENING CREDITS

The history of brewing begins with homebrew. Making beer for sale to others is a fairly recent phenomenon: In fact, for millennia, there was no beer industry at all. Beer was "liquid bread," that for most people was a form of sustenance rather than an intoxicant. However, every would-be brewer—whether working with a stovetop or in a warehouse—should know the history of beer making, especially the recent history of the band of homebrewers that came together to create the major *craft beer* brands you see on store shelves and in bars today.

BEER TIME TRAVEL: A BRIEF HISTORY OF BREWING AND HOMEBREWING

Beer was "discovered" anywhere between 10,000 and 4,000 BC (see timeline). Because fermentation predates recorded history, the exact date is unknown. The first beer brewers would have been inadvertent scientists who realized that their stored grains became sweeter if exposed to moisture and allowed to sprout. These sugary grains would have been both better tasting and easier to digest. But if left in liquid for too long, the sprouted grains would begin to ferment, and the fermented liquid could cause intoxication.

Early beer making can best be called an accidental art form. The science of brewing would come later, as humans began to realize that fermented drinks were healthier to drink than most of the available water, which was likely to contain harmful bacteria. It wasn't until the Middle Ages that the first "breweries" were created as *Trappist* monks in central

DID YOU KNOW?

The earliest surviving written record of beer making comes from clay tablets inscribed by the Sumerians, who thrived from about 5,500 to 1,750 BCE. They paid their workers in beer.

Europe began making beer as part of their daily duties. These monks kept careful records of their recipes and even began labeling their beer according to its strength, marking stronger brews with more Xs than weaker beer.

With the growing number of brewers came a proliferation in beer styles and ingredients, which in turn gave rise to some of the first laws governing how to brew beer. Beer legislation led to legislation restricting how alcoholic beverages could be made and—later—consumed. The most infamous legislation came in the form of Prohibition, which outlawed alcohol production and sales in many countries, including the United States.

The lasting effects of Prohibition included the consolidation of breweries, which reduced the variety of beer styles on the market. The world wars caused further deterioration in the beer marketplace, as many Americans rejected the predominant German-style *lagers* that they associated with Germany. By 1960, only 140 breweries remained in the United States.

Oddly, it was another war that helped launch the modern American craft beer movement. During the Vietnam War, many young people fled to Europe to avoid the draft. As a result, Americans became acquainted with beer styles that were not readily available in the United States. Back home after the war, a small band of homebrewers started replicating the beers they had loved while abroad, sharing recipes, and eventually forming their own *craft breweries*.

These early American craft beer makers were an industrious bunch. Many took on venture capitalists as partners, while others turned to *contract brewing* to turn a profit. Among the most successful of contract brewers was Boston Beer Company, producer of Samuel Adams beers. One of the company's cofounders, Jim Koch (pronounced "cook"), was a genius marketer who appealed to Americans' sense of patriotism. Today, Sam Adams remains one of the largest craft beer makers in the United States.

By 2014, the number of craft beer makers in the United States had skyrocketed to almost 3,500 breweries and brewpubs, which produced 11 percent of the country's beer (by volume).

DID YOU KNOW?
Frederick "Fritz" Maytag, the beer-loving heir to the appliance fortune, is widely considered the father of craft brewing. In 1965, he purchased San Francisco's Anchor Brewing Company, an old German brewery specializing in steam beer, and revived the style.

BEER TIMELINE

- 10,000 BCE – Nomadic hunting-gathering tribes establish permanent grain-growing settlements in the Fertile Crescent, which arced along the eastern shores of the Mediterranean Sea from present-day Egypt to Syria, and along the Tigris and Euphrates Rivers from present-day Turkey to Kuwait.

- 55 BCE – Roman legions carry beer into northern Europe.

- 822 CE – The first use of hops is recorded at a Trappist monastery in northern France.

- 1612 – Dutch explorer Adrian Block and colonist Hans Christiansen build what is believed to be the New World's first brewery, on the south end of Manhattan Island.

- 1620 – Arriving in North America aboard the *Mayflower*, the Pilgrims divert to Plymouth, Massachusetts, to disembark because of a shortage of provisions, including beer.

- 1857 – French scientist Louis Pasteur discovers the mechanisms of fermentation.

- 1862 – To raise funds for the impending Civil War, President Abraham Lincoln imposes a $1 per barrel excise tax on beer.

- 1919 – The 18th Amendment to the US Constitution is ratified, prohibiting "the manufacture, sale, or transportation of intoxicating liquors."

- 1933 – The 21st Amendment to the US Constitution is ratified, repealing the 18th Amendment.

- 1979 – President Jimmy Carter legalizes homebrewing; many states continue to prohibit brewing beer at home.

- 1991 – The United States becomes the world's largest beer producer, making 20 percent of the world's beer.

- 2013 – Mississippi becomes the 50th state in the United States to legalize homebrewing.

- 2014 – The Brewers Association announces the number of US breweries has passed 2,800.

TYPES OF BEER

Beer traditionally comes in two types: ale and lager. Some beers are harder to classify because they are ale-lager hybrids, taking some characteristics from lagers and others from ales. In addition, there is porter beer and its darker cousin, stout. Technically, these fall into the ale category, but they're distinctive enough to be considered an independent beer type. The categories of beer listed in the sidebars on the next few pages are based on the most recent *Beer Judge Certification Program (BJCP)* standards.

ALE CHARACTERISTICS

Ales are categorized according to their yeast and fermentation process. Ales are brewed with *top-fermenting* yeast at warmer—and in the case of saison beers, significantly warmer—temperatures than lagers, for a relatively short period of time. In fact, ales will ferment in as little as one week, making them idea for homebrewing.

Modern ale recipes came out of English and Belgian Trappist traditions, but they date back to earliest civilization. Ales are much more conducive to experimentation, as they can be made with more ingredients and still retain the qualities of that particular beer style. Ales typically

DID YOU KNOW?

Ale yeast ferment at relatively warm temperatures, mostly top-fermenting while floating at the top of your fermentation vessel. Ale yeast thrive in the upper 60s to low 70s degrees Fahrenheit range.

can be enjoyed at a variety of temperatures; many Americans visiting Great Britain are shocked by the warm beer served there (often from a cask, which offers minimal carbonation).

Ales vary widely in flavor: In some cases, one particularly robust flavor may overpower all the other flavors in a beer. Ales generally are very aromatic and often quite bitter, and the *alcohol by volume (ABV)* range is exceptionally broad. There are commercial breweries making ales with as little as 2.5 percent ABV, and craft experimenters taking theirs up to 20 percent ABV (and even higher). Ales typically have good *head retention* (i.e., more and longer-lasting foam) and range in color from pale straw to black (see Porter & Stout Characteristics, on page 28).

ALE CATEGORIES (76 TOTAL)

Note: Most of the recommended examples are widely distributed in the United States.

Belgian- and French-Origin Ale Styles (16 categories)

Belgian-Style Blonde Ale

Belgian-Style Dark Strong Ale

Belgian-Style Dubbel

Belgian-Style Flanders Oud Bruin or Oud Red Ale

Belgian-Style Fruit Lambic

Belgian-Style Gueuze Lambic

Belgian-Style Lambic

Belgian-Style Pale Ale

Belgian-Style Pale Strong Ale

Belgian-Style Quadrupel

Belgian-Style Table Beer

Belgian-Style Tripel

Belgian-Style White (or Wit)/ Belgian-Style Wheat

French & Belgian-Style Saison

French-Style Bière de Garde

Other Belgian-Style Ale

British-Origin Ale Styles (21 categories)

British-Style Barleywine Ale

British-Style Imperial Stout

Brown Porter

Classic English-Style Pale Ale

English-Style Brown Ale

English-Style Dark Mild Ale

English-Style India Pale Ale

English-Style Pale Mild Ale

English-Style Summer Ale

Extra Special Bitter

Oatmeal Stout

Old Ale

Ordinary Bitter

Robust Porter

Scotch Ale

Scottish-Style Export Ale

Scottish-Style Heavy Ale

Scottish-Style Light Ale

Special Bitter or Best Bitter

Strong Ale

Sweet Stout or Cream Stout

German-Origin Ale Styles (12 categories)

Bamberg-Style Weiss Rauchbier (smoked Helles or Dunkel)

Berliner-Style Weisse

German-Style Altbier

German-Style Kölsch/Köln-Style Kölsch

German-Style Leichtes Weizen/ Weissbier

Kellerbier/Zwickelbier (ale)

Leipzig-Style Gose

South German-Style Bernsteinfarbenes Weizen/ Weissbier

South German-Style Dunkel Weizen/Dunkel Weissbier

South German-Style Hefeweizen/ Hefeweissbier

South German-Style Kristal Weizen/Kristal Weissbier

South German-Style Weizenbock/Weissbock

Irish-Origin Ale Styles (3 categories)

Classic Irish-Style Dry Stout

Foreign (Export)-Style Stout

Irish-Style Red Ale

North American-Origin Ale Styles (19 categories)

American-Style Amber/Red Ale

American-Style Barleywine Ale

American-Style Black Ale

American-Style Brett Beer

American-Style Brown Ale

American-Style Imperial Porter

American-Style Imperial Stout

American-Style India Pale Ale

American-Style Pale Ale

American-Style Sour Ale

American-Style Stout

American-Style Strong Pale Ale

American-Style Wheatwine Ale

Dark American-Belgo-Style Ale

Golden or Blonde Ale

Imperial or Double India Pale Ale

Imperial or Double Red Ale

Pale American-Belgo-Style Ale

Smoked Porter

Other Origin Ale Styles (5 categories)

Adambier

Australian-Style Pale Ale

Dutch-Style Kuit

Grodziskie

International-Style Pale Ale

PORTER & STOUT CHARACTERISTICS

Porter is an ale that originated in 18th-century Britain. The ever-evolving brew was in many ways the first "modern" beer, in that it was brewed deliberately to standards. Drunk for millennia as a safer alternative to water, which was more likely to contain harmful or even deadly bacteria, most beer was "table" beer with a low ABV. By contrast, porter beer was conditioned and weighed in much heavier, meaning it had a higher ABV that aimed to intoxicate. It originated as an over-hopped English brown ale that was fermented for an extended period. The style continues to be tweaked and revised by brewers worldwide. Medium to very dark in color, it has moderate roasted malt flavors and chocolate or coffee tones. Its clarity ranges from good to nearly opaque, with a solid retention of its tan head.

DID YOU KNOW?

The amount of carbonation in beer can alter its style category. Certain styles of beer are expected to be more effervescent than other styles. For example, Belgian-style beers tend to be more highly carbonated than stouts.

Stout, originally "stout porter," was first brewed as a "light" porter, meaning that it had a low ABV. Stouts are typically super flavorful, with prominent roasted coffee flavors, often with chocolate and grain notes. With full body and high hop bitterness, the ABV of modern-day stouts can range from very low (oatmeal stout) to high (Russian imperial stout), and the range of flavors can go from malty-sweet to dry to bitter. Stouts can change flavor as they warm, and some beer drinkers prefer to drink them at room temperature. Stouts typically are opaque with a very creamy head.

LAGER CHARACTERISTICS

As with ales, lagers are categorized based on the yeast and fermentation process used in their brewing. Lagers are brewed with *bottom-fermenting* yeast at cooler temperatures than ales, generally taking several weeks to many months to ferment, depending on the ABV. Before refrigeration, lager beers were rare. Although *lagering* in caves dates back to the Middle Ages, it was only in the mid-1800s, when refrigeration became widespread, that lager beers came to dominate the European and American markets. Appropriately, lagers are typically served—and enjoyed—at colder temperatures.

Lager beers were particularly popular in central Europe, especially Germany, where *Reinheitsgebot*—beer purity laws—created a market for clean, crisp-tasting beers. Germans created many of the lager styles we drink (and homebrew) today, including bock beer, Märzen, helles, and Oktoberfest.

Lagers are known for their distinctive malt character and can range from pale straw to deep brown in color. While American palates have become trained to enjoy lagers (e.g., Budweiser, Coors), their popularity has more to do with balance than marketing. Lager beers can be very complex in their flavors, but typically no one flavor stands out in a lager.

DID YOU KNOW?

Lager yeast prefer relatively cool temperatures, mostly bottom-fermenting at the bottom of your fermentation vessel. Lager yeast work best in the high 40s to mid-50s degrees Fahrenheit range.

LAGER CATEGORIES (30 TOTAL)

European-Germanic-Origin Lager Styles (18 categories)

Bamberg-Style Bock Rauchbier

Bamberg-Style Helles Rauchbier

Bamberg-Style Märzen Rauchbier

Bohemian-Style Pilsner

Dortmunder/European-Style Export

European Low-Alcohol Lager/German Leicht (bier)

European-Style Dark/Münchner Dunkel

German-Style Doppelbock

German-Style Eisbock

German-Style Heller Bock/Maibock

German-Style Märzen

German-Style Oktoberfest/Wiesen

German-Style Pilsner

German-Style Schwarzbier

Kellerbier/Zwickelbier (lager)

Münchner-Style Helles

Traditional German-Style Bock

Vienna-Style Lager

North American-Origin Lager Styles (9 categories)

American-Style Amber (Low-Calorie) Lager

American-Style Amber Lager

American-Style Dark Lager

American-Style Ice Lager

American-Style Lager

American-Style Light (Low-Calorie) and Low-Carbohydrate Lager

American-Style Malt Liquor

American-Style Märzen/Oktoberfest

American-Style Pilsner

Other Origin Lager Styles (3 categories)

Australasian, Latin American, or Tropical-Style Light Lager

Baltic-Style Porter

International-Style Pilsner

MIXED/HYBRID CHARACTERISTICS

Many beers don't strictly fall into the lager or ale category. Beer types are defined by yeast and brewing techniques, but some "lagers" are brewed more like traditional ales, and vice versa.

Among the better known hybrid beers:

BARLEYWINE A high-ABV "warming beer" that originated in England. US brewers have recently been adding significant amounts of hops, creating a distinctive American barleywine style. A barleywine served at the proper temperature (i.e., not chilled) will have brilliant clarity and an off-white head with limited retention. At cooler temperatures, there can be a *chill haze*. A variation made with wheat, called wheatwine, tends to be less sweet than traditional barleywine. Recommended beers in this style: Ridgeway Criminally Bad Elf, Heavy Seas Beer Below Decks Barleywine Style Ale, Sierra Nevada Bigfoot, and Avery Hog Heaven Dry-Hopped Barleywine Style Ale.

DID YOU KNOW?

Each style of beer has a set acceptable color range; beers outside this range are considered a different style. Colors have been assigned numbers according to the *Standard Reference Method (SRM)*: Low numbers indicate lighter-colored malts/beers; higher numbers indicate darker malts/beers.

FRENCH ALE French farmhouse ale styles, including bière de garde (sometimes called a bière de mars in Northern France), which is similar to Belgian saison (see *Saison* entry on page 34). Typically copper in color, they have a relatively high ABV (in the 8.5 to 10 percent range). These beers age well and were traditionally stored in corked bottles in cellars for an extended period of time. They have prominent malty and sometimes fruity flavors, with some *caramelization*. Clarity is generally poor, with a typically lasting haze. However, the solid white foam head has quite good retention. There are three main variations: blonde, brune, and ambrée (blond, brown, and amber). Recommended beers in this style: Brasserie St. Germain Page 24's Bière de Printemps and the beers from Brasserie La Choulette.

GERMAN KELLERBIER An "unfinished" beer that originated in German rathskellers (cellar bars; *kellerbier* translates to "cellar beer"). Unfiltered and unpasteurized, this beer is a low-carbonation lager with a full body, a balanced malt flavor with bready tones, and a slight haze. The clarity should still be bright, but head retention is minimal. It's also known as zwickelbier. Recommended beers in this style: Mahrs-Bräu Ungespundet-Hefetrüb, Mikkeller Wet Hop Kellerbier, and Samuel Adams Alpine Spring.

SMOKED BEER A German-style beer brewed from malted barley that's been dried (smoked) over an open flame. With a very low hop profile, the flavor of this beer falls along a continuum from sweet (i.e., malty) to smoky. Although ales, usually porters, can be made from smoked malt, the rauchbier, a lager, is the most traditional smoked beer. Smoked beer is generally an amber-colored brew, with good clarity and a moderate tan- or cream-colored head. Recommended beer in this style: Aecht Schlenkerla Rauchbier Märzen.

HYBRID/MIXED LAGER AND ALE CATEGORIES (35 TOTAL)

Aged Beer
American-Style Cream Ale
American-Style Fruit Beer
Belgian-Style Fruit Beer
California Common (Steam) Beer
Chocolate/Cocoa-Flavored Beer
Coffee-Flavored Beer
Dark American Wheat Beer with or without Yeast
Experimental Beer
Field Beer
Fresh- or Wet-Hop Beer
Fruit Wheat Beer with or without Yeast
German-Style Rye Ale (Roggenbier) with or without Yeast
Gluten-Free Beer
Herb and/or Spice Beer
Historical Beer

Indigenous/Regional Beer
Japanese Sake-Yeast Beer
Light American Wheat Beer with or without Yeast
Non-Alcoholic (Beer)/Malt Beverage
Other Strong Ale or Lager
Pumpkin Beer
Rye Beer with or without Yeast
Session Beer
Smoked Beer
Specialty Beer
Specialty Honey Beer
Wild Beer
Wood- and/or Barrel-Aged Beer
Wood- and/or Barrel-Aged Dark Beer
Wood- and/or Barrel-Aged Pale to Amber Beer
Wood- and/or Barrel-Aged Strong Beer
Wood- and/or Barrel-Aged Sour Beer

STYLES OF BEER

AMBER This beer style typically encompasses four popular types of ale and lager: altbier, kölsch, Märzen (Oktoberfest), and Vienna lager. Amber to copper in color, this beer has clean character, bright clarity, and moderate to no head retention. The flavor is crisp and mildly hopped with a nice malt balance. The altbier is an ale that ferments at cooler temperatures, like a lager. The kölsch is a lager that ferments at higher temperatures, like an ale. Märzen, a lager, was historically made to age, with a higher ABV and moderate bitterness from the addition of extra hops, a preservative. Vienna lager is similar in flavor; in Germany, both are traditionally imbibed at the end of harvest season as part of the famous Oktoberfest. Recommended beers in this style: Otter Creek Copper Ale, Long Trail Brewing Co. Ale, Goose Island Summertime, Left Hand Brewing Company Oktoberfest, Blue Point Toasted Lager, Negra Modelo, and Brooklyn Lager.

BLONDE ALE These ales were created as "gateway" craft beers. Similar in style to a German kölsch, blonde ales were the earliest craft beers, and offer up crisp, mild, well-balanced, and malty flavors. Blonde ale is a smooth, "drinkable" beer with clean fermentation free of haze and yeast notes with no overpowering flavors. Recommended beers in this style: Pete's Wicked Ale and Goose Island Blonde Ale.

BROWN ALE Both the American and English varieties of brown ale tend to be malty with a toffee or caramel finish and occasional coffee or chocolate notes. The key differences between the American and English varieties are that the American version has a more pronounced hop profile that adds bitterness, and it has more carbonation. A brown ale should have good clarity and average head retention. Recommended beers in this style: Brooklyn Brown Ale, Bell's Best Brown, Theakston Traditional, and Samuel Smith's Nut Brown Ale.

CREAM ALE This "American special" ale is fermented at the "wrong" temperature. Cream ale, which came out of Canada following Prohibition, is fermented longer and cooler, like a lager; it has a sweetness reminiscent of the flavor of corn (or corn sugar), low bitterness, and ample carbonation. Cream ales are straw to gold in color with good clarity and a slight white head. Recommended beers in this style: Laughing Dog Cream Ale and Genesee Cream Ale.

DARK LAGER This category includes Munich dunkel and schwarzbier. The Munich malt it's brewed with offers up a rich flavor with a bready quality, and the beer has a low, but present, hop bitterness. Dark lagers still have excellent clarity and strong head retention. Recommended beers in this style: Penn Dark Lager, Löwenbräu Dunkel, Shiner Bock, Samuel Adams Black Lager, and Ayinger Altbairisch Dunkel.

FRUIT BEER This beer style can range from the funky (lambic) to the inventive (traditional recipes with fruit added). Lambic beers are made via intentional contamination with *wild yeast* (e.g., *Brettanomyces*) and bacteria (e.g., *Lactobacillus, Pediococcus*) during the fermentation process. These beers are typically tart, complex, sour ales. Fruit—most often citrus—can also be added to the *boil* or the fermenter to add flavor to the beer. Recommended beers in this style: Great South Bay Brewery's Blood Orange Pale Ale, Bud Light Lime, and the line of lambics by Lindemans.

GOLDEN LAGER The beer you probably grew up with, American lager is known more for how it doesn't taste than how it does: minimal aromas, no prominent flavors, typically well balanced, and crisp. These lagers have the palest straw color and great clarity, with generally strong head retention. These beers are *sessionable*, i.e., good for quaffing (or, admittedly, chugging), because they tend to be very refreshing and low in alcohol. Recommended beers in this style: Pabst Blue Ribbon, Narragansett, Budweiser, and Coors (Original).

INDIA PALE ALE Among the fastest growing segments of the craft beer market, IPA is a highly hopped, extremely aromatic beer. American IPAs tend to be far more bitter than their English predecessors, with moderately to extremely assertive flavors, such as notes of grapefruit and pine. Among the most persistent of false tales is that of IPA's origin. The story goes that beer shipped from England to British troops stationed in India in the 1800s was highly hopped to prevent it from spoiling on the long journey. In fact, the army was drinking porters, and it was the British navy that preferred pale ale. Historians speculate that the IPA originated with pale ale that was brewed at sea by sailors experimenting with higher alcohol levels. It's possible that they added extra hops, or that the constant, extreme motion of ships under sail resulted in this new version of the traditional pale ale.

LIGHT The "light" beers marketed today are lower-calorie and lower-ABV versions of mass-market brewers' standard lagers, for instance. Typically pale in color, light beers are known for their absence of strong flavors. Hop presence tends to be low to none, both in taste and aroma. Great for quaffing, they are fresh and quick-drinking brews enjoyed very cold. Also in this category are some hybrid ales, such as cream ale. Recommended beers in this style: Bud Light and Sam Adams Light.

PALE ALE This is simply the common name for hop-forward, copper-colored ales. With their strong citrus aroma, these beers tend to have mild malt character and a dry finish. Clarity ranges from good to nearly opaque. The tan head has good retention. Recommended beers in this style: Sierra Nevada Pale Ale, Firestone Walker Pale Ale, and Lagunitas Pale Ale.

PILSNER Originating in the Czech city of Plzen (Pilsen), pilsner is a lager with extreme clarity, good head retention, and spicy floral notes. It's made with noble hops (one of the four hop varieties—Tettnanger, Spalt, Hallertauer, and

DID YOU KNOW?
Although it's perceived somewhat subjectively, a beer's intensity affects its style. The stronger or more pronounced a characteristic, the more intense it's considered. Intensity can be used to describe aroma, body, flavor, and bitterness/sweetness, among other qualities.

Saaz—that grow in Central Europe). Its color ranges from pale to golden yellow. Depending on where it's brewed, it may be spelled "pilsener" (in the Czech Republic, for example); the beer is also called "pils." It's one of the world's most popular beer styles. Recommended beers in this style: Pilsner Urquell, Victory Prima Pils, Bitburger, and Brooklyn Pilsner.

RED ALE While some American amber beers are labeled "red," red ale is actually a sour beer that originated in the Flanders region of Belgium. As with fruit beers, red ale is fermented with Lactobacillus and is known for intense fruit overtones and strong aromas. Because of their high concentration of tannins, red ales are often described as "wine-like." Recommended beers in this style: Petrus Oud Bruin and the line of beers from Rodenbach.

SAISON A Belgian pale ale made with its own unique yeast, saison is notable for its fruity aroma and spicy complexity. Hop flavors are occasionally noticeable, but most prominent is the beer's Champagne-like finish. Clarity ranges from good to poor (haze is acceptable in this style). Head retention is minimal. Saison is now popular on both sides of the Atlantic, with many quality entries from US craft brewers. Recommended beers in this style: Dupont, Ommegang Hennepin, Jolly Pumpkin Bam Bière, and Stillwater Artisanal Ales Stateside Saison.

STRONG ALE Typically an English- or Scottish-style ale, this beer is usually fruity, malty, nutty, and high in alcohol (ABV can exceed 12 percent). It's one of the few beer styles for which a strong alcohol flavor isn't considered a fault; strong ale is often described as a "warming" beer. The beer has good clarity and a sturdy, creamy head. It pairs very well with strong cheeses in the English tradition. Recommended beers in this style: Founders Dirty Bastard, George Gale & Co., Gale's Prize Old Ale, and Theakston Old Peculier.

WHEAT BEER A protein-rich beer with a tell-tale haze, wheat beer originated in Germany, where weissbier continues to be a popular style. Wheat beers use a large proportion (typically 50 percent) of wheat alongside malted barley. In Belgium, the beer is known as witbier; in the United States, the beers tend to be hoppier and are called wheat ales. Pale straw to dark gold in color, wheat beers typically have poor clarity (haze is acceptable in this style). Head retention is generally strong. Other wheat beers include Berliner Weisse, dunkleweizen, gose, hefeweizen, and weizenbock. Recommended beers in this style: Allagash White, The Bruery Hottenroth Berliner Weisse, Hitachino White, Ommegang Witte, and Ayinger Bräu-Weisse.

DID YOU KNOW?
Original Gravity (OG), the amount of sugar in wort before yeast are added, determines its fermentability and is one of the keys to a beer's style (and ABV). The difference between OG and post-fermentation final gravity (FG) determines ABV.

MASTER TIPS

In 1983, smaller craft brewers united in an attempt to distinguish themselves from the big operations, whose products, they claimed, were not true craft beers. The craft-brewing industry's main guild, the Association of Brewers, drafted a definition of *craft brewery*, and its successor, the Brewers Association (BA), continues to tweak the formula. The designation currently includes three components:

1. Small: Craft brewery production is currently limited to 15,000 barrels per year for a microbrewery and up to 6 million for a giant craft brewery.

2. Independent: At least 75 percent of a craft brewery must be owned by craft brewers whose primary financial interest is in craft beer, not by shareholders, non-craft brewers, or non-beer businesses.

3. Traditional: Craft brewers ferment beer from traditional or innovative brewing ingredients; flavored malt beverages (beer-based drinks such as "hard lemonade" and "coolers") are not considered craft beer.

Lumping together brewers that make 15,000 barrels a year with those that make 6 million barrels a year may seem ludicrous at first glance, but a number of craft beer pioneers have remained independent and traditional while experiencing tremendous growth. Two or three of them produce more than one million barrels per year, and the largest, Boston Beer Company, sold just shy of three million barrels in 2012. Compare that to the sales of the "Big Two" mega-brewers, Anheuser-Busch InBev and MillerCoors, which together sold close to 160 million barrels during the same period.

Craft brewers, however, have made an impact on the megabrewers: The big are getting smaller, and the small are getting bigger. In 2012, the sales of the Big Two dropped 6 percent by volume, while craft brew sales rose 15 percent by volume. As a result, more small craft breweries are being bought out by the mega-breweries (the first purchase of note was in 2011 when AB-InBev purchased Chicago's renowned Goose Island Brewery for a reported $38.8 million). In 2013, there were 2,768 craft breweries in the United States, and more than one brewery per day was scheduled to come on line in 2014.

3

HOMEBREWING BASICS

As a homebrewer, you'll be working with the four main ingredients in beer: water, malt, yeast, and hops. Historically, many other ingredients have been added, and hops—now considered a key ingredient—have only been used since the 9th century, a relatively recent date in beer history. Without water, a cereal grain, and yeast, a beverage can't be called beer. Without malt and hops, a beverage wouldn't be recognized as beer by most beer drinkers today (with apologies to gluten-free sorghum-based beers). Each of the four key beer ingredients plays a different role in brewing. A solid understanding of this quartet will make you a better homebrewer.

THE JOYS OF HOMEBREWING

Hopefully by now, you've had the chance to make, taste, and review your first homebrewed beer. There were probably things you liked about it and things you didn't. Brewing beer is a process, and the more you understand about what goes into making your beer, the better the beer ultimately will be.

INGREDIENTS

MALTS AND SUGARS

The very first step in the brewing process is *malting/milling*. Only the very best "brew-grade" barley is malted. The process of malting begins when the grain—usually barley, but sometimes corn, oats, rice, rye, and sorghum, among others—is steeped in water for about two days until it germinates, developing various proteins and enzymes. Germination is halted by heat, in a process called kilning. The malt may then be toasted, or roasted, to develop its flavor further. The more toasted the malt used in brewing, the darker the beer. Milling crushes the malt to exactly the right consistency to maximize the release of *maltose*, a sugar that yeast love to eat, during brewing. Malt typically comes in the following forms:

KILNED MALT (BASE MALT OR LAGER MALT) Nearly all malts are kilned at a temperature of about 100°F for an extended period of time (at least 24 hours). Kilning stops the germination of the grain without causing much change in the color of the grain. Pale ale and pilsner are made from kilned malt.

TOASTED MALT *Base malt* is heated to create a darker, mildly "toasty" flavor. Among other beers made with toasted malt are bocks and porters.

KILNED-AND-ROASTED MALT The combination of kilning and roasting brings in coffee, dark chocolate, and "burnt" flavors to a malt. These malts are used sparingly in dark beers. Be aware that a little goes a long way: Kilned-and-roasted malts can overwhelm the flavor of your beer if you use too much.

ROASTED MALT Roasting causes caramelization, yielding malts that are sometimes referred to as caramel malts or *crystal malts*.

HOPS

Hops are the conical female flowers of the *Humulus lupulus* vine, which is called a "bine." The resin-rich cones give beer its distinctive aroma and flavor. Hops serve three purposes in beer: to enhance aroma, intensify bitterness, and add flavor. Certain hop varieties are best as bittering agents because of their higher percentage of alpha acid resin (noted on the label), while other varieties are high in aromatic oils. Freshness is key to the potency of hops: Store your hops in an airtight container in a cool place (between 50°F and 60°F).

Hops come in different forms:

DRY HOPS Whole, dried cones that are added to the wort late in the *boil* are excellent in *dry hopping*. They present a stronger aroma than other hop forms.

FRESH HOPS Hops that are fresh off the bine and neither dried nor processed are also known as green hops. They lend a more subtle bitterness and are excellent for adding aroma.

HOP EXTRACT Liquid essence of hops can be used in place of dried hop forms.

HOP PELLETS Processed from powdered cones, these look like animal feed. One pound of dried hop cones yields about 10 ounces of pellets. Pellets store well and are easy to weigh, but they turn to sludge in the wort, making for tedious straining.

HOP PLUGS Whole cones can be dried and compressed into a plug shape. They remain fresh longer than whole hops and are easier to measure, but they also soak up wort.

Whatever types of hops you use, their impact on your beer's flavor has a lot to do with timing:

> longer boil = more bitterness, less aroma
> shorter boil = more aroma, less bitterness
> no boil (i.e., dry hopping) = aroma only

YEAST

Yeast deal with the cool side of brewing: fermentation. Even "warm" fermentation for ales or saisons, which can ferment at temperatures approaching 90°F, is cool in comparison to a boiling wort.

When yeast go to work, they digest sugar and create carbon dioxide and ethanol (alcohol) as byproducts. Yeast also make more yeast, which, in turn, make more alcohol. Some species of yeast are best for brewing ale, whereas others are suited to lager. Any yeast can generate alcohol, but different strains produce unique flavor compounds.

Although yeast can work on their own for the most part, they do need some tending. If you don't take care of yeast, they easily perish and quit making beer. Yeast typically need four things to survive: oxygen; sugar; nutrients such as nitrogen, minerals, and vitamins; and a hospitable temperature. When you aerate your wort, you're ensuring your yeast have enough oxygen. As for sugar and nutrients, the maltose in your wort will meet all of your yeast's needs. Various strains of yeast run hotter or cooler, so you must keep an eye on recommended fermentation temperatures.

There are many varieties of yeast available from labs and retailers around the world. As a beginning homebrewer, you should stick with simple, dry brewer's yeast. The alternative is to use liquid yeast, which is more expensive and somewhat harder to pitch. It's true that a significantly wider variety of yeast strains are available in liquid as opposed to dry form, so you can do a lot of really interesting things with liquid yeast. However, dry yeast will serve you well 90 percent of the time.

HERBS AND OTHER INGREDIENTS

Beyond the key beer ingredients of water, malt, yeast, and hops, you can add almost anything edible to your brew (see more on experimenting with ingredients in chapter 5). Some of the more common beer *additives* include the following:

FRUITS AND VEGETABLES From stone fruits and berries to pumpkin and jalapeño peppers, fruits and vegetables can put some wild and delightful spins on a standard brew.

HERBS Like hops, herbs fall into three categories—bittering, flavoring, and aromatic—and are added to the brew on a similar schedule. Use fresh herbs, not dried. Good options for bittering, added at the beginning of the boil, are dandelion, sage, milk thistle, and nettle. Hearty-flavoring herbs, which you add 30 to 40 minutes before completion of the boil, include rosemary, oregano, and mint. More delicate-flavoring herbs, such as marjoram, lemon balm, and thyme, may be added in the final 15 minutes. Aromatic herbs that are best added after the boil include lavender, chamomile, and elderflower. Experiment with other herbs as well, but use small quantities until you get a sense of their effect on your brew.

IRISH MOSS Available in homebrew shops, Irish moss is a *fining agent* rather than a flavoring. It thoroughly clarifies cloudy beer. Haziness is a common problem for homebrewers, and an easy way to eliminate it is to add Irish moss near the end of the boil.

SPICES Add spices at the start of the boil to bring out their flavor and near the end of the boil to bring out their aroma. Spices commonly added to beer include cinnamon, dried peppercorns, and dried citrus peels. Whole spices, as opposed to ground, work best, and the fresher the better. Roots (e.g., licorice) should be dried before using.

EQUIPMENT

Step into a homebrewing store or click around an online forum, and you may end up thinking, "Look at all this stuff I have to buy." In reality, you don't have to buy a lot of paraphernalia to get started as a homebrewer. Whether you consider yourself the next top chef or you just like cooking at home, you may already have a lot of equipment that you can use as or convert into brewing gear. Some equipment is required, some is optional, and all equipment can be scaled for both casual and professional homebrew setups.

HOMEBREWING EQUIPMENT CATEGORIES AND DESCRIPTIONS

EQUIPMENT FOR BREWING (REQUIRED)

AIRLOCK This device is used during fermentation to allow the carbon dioxide released by yeast to escape the fermenter while not allowing air back in; outside air could contaminate the beer or cause it to oxidize. Airlocks come in bubbler and three-piece styles.

BREW POT(S) As a beginning brewer, choose a stockpot or similar vessel made of stainless steel or ceramic-coated steel. For the 2½-gallon recipes in this book, the pot must be able to hold a minimum of 3 gallons. For a 5-gallon batch, you'll want a pot that can hold at least 8 gallons. If you don't plan to use a *lauter tun*, you'll also need a second pot of the same size when brewing all-grain recipes.

FERMENTER Use a fermenting vessel that will allow the yeast to expand and give off carbon dioxide but that's not too much bigger than the batch you're brewing, so the air space at the top of the fermenter is minimized. For a 2½-gallon batch, use a 3-gallon food-grade plastic pail or a 3-gallon glass or plastic carboy. If you choose a carboy, you'll need a blowoff hose in addition to an airlock (see page 42). A 5-gallon batch requires a 5-gallon fermenter.

LIDS FOR BREW POT AND FERMENTER Some containers must be covered and some may be covered. You'll need lids for both.

RACKING CANE You'll need a rigid plastic tube with a sediment stand-off (i.e., a part attached to the tip to draw liquid in from half an inch or so above the end of the cane) to siphon off wort while leaving trub and hops debris behind. Some models are equipped with a pump to help start the flow of liquid.

SANITIZER It's absolutely essential to use a food-grade sanitizer when brewing.

SPOON OR STIRRING PADDLE A food-grade plastic utensil is used to stir the wort during boiling.

THERMOMETER Buy a thermometer that has a wide temperature range (32°F to 212°F) and that's responsive enough to detect temperature within 10 seconds. Dial thermometers and floating dairy thermometers work very well. A candy thermometer will work at higher temperatures during the boil, but it won't work for monitoring fermentation.

TUBING Food-grade plastic tubing is used in siphoning and bottling; make sure to purchase the right diameter to fit your racking cane, *bottle filler*, or other equipment.

Homebrewing equipment (clockwise from top left): airlocks (bubbler and three-piece type), bottling bucket, siphon with racking cane and bottle filler attachment, hydrometer, thermometers, fermenters (carboy and bucket with airlock)

EQUIPMENT FOR BOTTLING (REQUIRED)

BOTTLES The recipes in this book make enough beer for a standard case (i.e., 24 12-ounce bottles). You can also use 15 large-format (i.e., 22-ounce beer or 750-milliliter Champagne) bottles or about 18 swing-top 16-ounce bottles. Dark brown bottles are preferable to green or clear glass. You can clean and save used beer bottles; if you choose swing-tops, be sure to use new gaskets).

BOTTLE CAPPER Hand-held cappers are standard; bench cappers, which stand on a work surface, are somewhat easier to use and are necessary for larger bottles, especially Champagne bottles. Bench cappers typically are more than twice as expensive as hand cappers.

BOTTLE CAPS You can buy these by the bag. Standard caps are sufficient, although oxygen-absorbing crown caps are available.

Homebrewing equipment (clockwise from top left): mash tun, lauter tun, mesh bag, turkey baster or wine thief, tubing clamp

SIPHON You can use plain, food-grade plastic tubing, or a premade version that includes a racking cane and a bottle filler.

OTHER EQUIPMENT (OPTIONAL)

ALUMINUM FOIL This is used for covering ingredients; be sure to sanitize as necessary.

BLOWOFF HOSE See Glossary.

BOTTLE BRUSH A long-handled, narrow brush that makes bottle cleaning much easier. Extra-large versions are available for cleaning carboys.

BOTTLE FILLER See Glossary.

BOTTLING BUCKET See Glossary.

CAN OPENER For canned ingredients such as LME.

DIGITAL SCALE For convenient and accurate measuring, especially if you buy ingredients in bulk.

FUNNEL Any food-grade funnel will work, but you might want to insert a funnel screen to catch residue from hops and additives. Funnels come in a variety of diameters from 4 to 10 inches; a larger funnel helps reduce splashing and spilling when handling large amounts of liquid.

GLASS MEASURING CUP A quart-size, heat-resistant measuring cup is helpful for everything from transferring ingredients to rehydrating yeast.

HYDROMETER See page 42.

ICE Buy it if you can't make enough ice on your own. However, be aware that some commercial ice has additives that can affect the temperature during wort cooling.

LAUTER TUN See Glossary.

MASH TUN See Glossary.

MESH BAG Mashing or dry hopping hops with your ingredients in a mesh bag helps keep them from creating a mess while mashing or fermenting, and it reduces or eliminates the need for straining.

PLASTIC BUCKET OR GARBAGE PAIL A heavy-duty food-grade container is recommended for mixing your sanitizer, transferring wort, and general brewing needs.

PLASTIC WRAP This is used for covering ingredients; be sure it's clean and doesn't get contaminated as you tear it.

POTHOLDERS Brew pots get hot. Enough said.

SCISSORS You'll need to cut open packets of ingredients; remember to sanitize if you are cutting open anything that will touch the wort, such as liquid yeast.

TOWELS Clean towels or paper towels will come in handy for spills; be careful not to get contaminants on your brew pot by using a dirty towel.

TUBING CLAMP See Glossary.

TURKEY BASTER OR WINE THIEF See Glossary.

WHAT'S A HYDROMETER?

The easiest way to know for sure when your beer has fermented to the right point—that is, when it has the level of alcohol you desire—is to use a *hydrometer*. This handy, affordable tool measures the *specific gravity*, aka *gravity,* of water-based liquids. At any stage of the game, float the calibrated glass tube in a sample of your beverage-in-progress, then determine its alcohol level by comparing its specific gravity with that of water itself. Pure water has a specific gravity of 1.000. Full of dissolved sugars and other substances, unfermented wort is "thicker" than water, with a gravity greater than that of water. This is a beer's original gravity (OG).

Partially converted to alcohol by fermentation, beer is "thinner" than wort, with a gravity less than the OG but still greater than water's gravity. For the purpose of determining your beer's alcohol by volume—its ABV—at any point during fermentation, this is called *final gravity (FG)*.

Enter your OG and FG into a simple formula, and you can find out its ABV:

$$(OG - FG) \times 131 = ABV$$

For example, if your original gravity is 1.080 and your final gravity is 1.011, your ABV is:

$$1.080 - 1.011 = 0.069 \times 131 = 9.039\%$$

This isn't the most precise ABV formula, just as the hydrometer isn't the most precise instrument, but it will give you a reasonably accurate figure.

When you're making a style of beer that's supposed to have a particular ABV, a hydrometer is an essential tool, especially if you're planning to enter your homebrew in a competition. ABV measurement is interesting and useful even if you're brewing just for fun, but like the brewers of centuries and millennia past, you can make beer without a hydrometer. And note that for the most part, a hydrometer is not particularly useful in monitoring the progress of all-extract beer recipes.

PROFESSIONAL EQUIPMENT

Perhaps, like so many homebrewers before you, you dream of expanding your operation and possibly becoming a commercial brewer yourself. If you've outgrown your 5-gallon fermenter, you might consider taking your homebrewing to the next level.

To get the most bang for your buck in equipment upgrades, buy a dedicated refrigerator and a kegging system. Once you get around to kegging your beers, you won't need as much space for bottle storage, and you can reserve your bottles for beers you'd like to keep for extended bottle conditioning. Adding a dedicated refrigeration unit to your brewing arsenal is the first step to expansion. A dorm-type mini-refrigerator or an old freezer set at a warmer-than-freezing temperature is possibly the best investment you can make to improve the quality of your beer. Be sure to add thermometers to your fermenter (many fermenters come with an internal thermometer) and the inside of your refrigerator. Don't be afraid to go cheap with this purchase; a lot of used refrigerators are discarded because they no longer stay cold enough, which makes them perfect for fermenting beer.

Alternatively, you can get a small refrigerator for as little as $80 at most big-box appliance stores. You might also consider getting a kegerator for a starting price of about $300. To become a master homebrewer, you need to limit inconsistencies in your beer. Proper refrigeration and temperature control will help you replicate your own recipes and ready them for retail.

Budget will undoubtedly determine how fast your brewing operation will grow. It's difficult to call yourself a "professional brewer" without at least a three-barrel system, which when new can cost upwards of $50,000. Most nanobrewers going pro begin just by brewing more with their existing homebrew system or building a bigger system from used equipment.

SANITATION

Some people are surprised when they realize just how much cleaning is a part of brewing. Walk into any brewery, and you'll see people in rubber boots wrangling mops, brooms, and hoses. Professional brewers spend more time cleaning than they do creating recipes and brewing. In fact, most brewers would agree that cleaning is the main part of brewing.

You probably don't love to clean, but if you want to end up with the beer you set out to brew, cleanliness is essential. The easiest way to ruin a batch of beer is through contamination in the cooking process. It's certainly possible to brew an award-winning beer in less than two hours, but it's highly unlikely that you will unless your equipment is completely clean before you get started. Everything that comes in contact with your ingredients, particularly after the wort has finished boiling, must be sanitized. Not just cleaned—sanitized.

Don't forget to sanitize the random pieces of equipment that will come in contact with your post-boil wort, such as lids, foil, strainers, funnels, airlocks, and racking canes. You probably won't forget to clean and sanitize your fermenter, but you might not remember to sanitize the spigot on your bottling bucket.

LET IT SHINE

It's important to understand that in homebrewing, there's more to cleaning than cleaning. There are three ways to prepare your equipment for action: cleaning, sanitizing, and sterilizing.

CLEANING This is how you remove residue and grime from your cooking area and brewing equipment. You probably have a great deal of experience cleaning because you wash your dishes, launder your clothes, and shower. Typically, you'll do your brew-cleaning with good old soap and water. You don't have to get fancy. Hot water and a neutral, unscented ("green," if you prefer) dish soap is typically all you need to clean your equipment; percarbonates such as OxiClean are especially good for hard-to-reach places like the insides of tubing. Everything you brew with should be cleaned before you start your brew day. For that matter, everything you brew with should also be cleaned at the end of your brew day. Assuming you don't live in a high-pollen or high-dust zone and your equipment is stored properly—boxed or bagged in a clean place—it should remain clean between brew days.

SANITIZING This is where you disinfect your equipment. You can't disinfect dirt, so you've got to clean before you sanitize. Every piece of equipment that touches your wort post-boil must be sanitized. Sanitizing reduces the risk that unwanted bacteria and yeast will get into your wort, which would compromise your control of the brewing process. Thanks to the homebrewing boom, there are a lot of excellent sanitation products on the market. Once upon a time, sanitizing chemicals were so toxic, you wouldn't want them to come in contact with your skin, let alone the equipment used to prepare beer you were going to drink. Now there are cheap and easy-to-use nontoxic (or less-toxic) alternatives that don't require post-sanitation cleaning. (A fun note: you can sanitize your bottle caps in vodka. However, never mix chemicals.) Among the main sanitizers are the following:

- Bleach—Although not the preferred sanitation product, household bleach can do the job in a recommended solution of 1 tablespoon of bleach for each gallon of water. Bleach is best when used on glass or plastics, but it should never be used on stainless steel. After bleaching, rinse your equipment in an electric dishwasher or under plenty of hot water without detergent.

- Iodophor—This iodine-based sanitizer is similar to bleach, but it's safe to use on stainless steel.

- PBW—This brand of commercial percarbonate is slightly more effective and quite a bit more expensive than a household percarbonate. If you'd like to clean out your deep pockets, go for this brand.

- Percarbonate—Good in tight spots, it can also remove bottle labels. Soak your bottles overnight in a solution of 1 tablespoon percarbonate to 2 gallons water, and the labels will slip right off. The most popular brand is OxiClean.

- Star San—A miracle sanitizer, this food-grade phosphoric acid is nontoxic: The chemical is the same cleanser found in toothpaste. It can be added to your wort with no consequence, and its brief contact time (it takes less than one minute for equipment to be fully sanitized) and long shelf-life (if mixed with distilled water, it will keep for months) make this the current first choice for most homebrewers. Saniclean is a low-foaming alternative that's slightly less effective than Star San.

STERILIZING Somewhat different than sanitizing, this process eradicates all microorganisms from your equipment. You aren't performing surgery, so you don't need to go overboard with sterilization. Most homebrewers don't do much sterilizing unless they want to grow and maintain yeast cultures. However, some prefer to sterilize, rather than sanitize, their bottles, which isn't a bad idea. For the homebrewer, there's really only one option when it's time to sterilize: heat. If you want to sterilize your bottles or equipment and you have an automatic dishwasher, you're in luck. Put your cleaned and sanitized items in the dishwasher with the drying function turned to "on" (i.e., don't use the energy-saving mode). Do a full wash with no detergent or rinse agent. (Bottle caps can also be sterilized by boiling.) The other option is to apply dry heat using your oven. Just be sure that anything you're heating is oven safe: Most bottles are not; anything that's Pyrex is oven safe, as are most metals. Equipment can be sterilized with dry heat in as little as one hour at 338°F. To preserve a microbe-free environment for your beer, handle your equipment carefully after it has been sterilized. You can cover sterilized containers with sanitized foil to keep contaminants from settling into them.

ANOTHER AREA OF CAUTION: When planning your cleaning strategy, you must take into account the materials of the equipment you use to make beer. You'll probably be cleaning and sanitizing three different materials: plastic, glass, and metal. Not every cleaner, and especially not every sanitizer, is appropriate for all of these materials. Even the materials themselves will probably not be identical.

GLASS If every piece of brewing equipment were made of glass, you'd probably never have to worry about cleanliness. Soap, hot water, and Star San are all you need to clean and sanitize glass, with bottle brushes strongly recommended for getting through the narrow openings of bottles and carboys. If there's mold inside either, use a bleach solution (1 tablespoon bleach to 1 gallon water) prior to cleaning and sanitizing.

METAL Brewing equipment is made with a wide variety of metals. Different metals have different tolerances for cleaning and sanitizing chemicals. The metals typically used in brewing include aluminum (brew pots; mash and lauter tuns) and stainless steel (kegs). Copper and brass are frequently used in commercial breweries. Chlorine dissolves the protective coating on stainless steel, so don't use bleach on it. Many household cleaners also contain chlorine, so use caution when cleaning metal equipment. Percarbonate is safe for aluminum and stainless steel.

PLASTIC You'll have three different kinds of plastic to clean and sterilize: food-grade high-density polyethylene plastic (utensils, fermenter), hard plastic (racking cane), and flexible plastic—actually, vinyl—tubing (siphon). The main concern with plastic is that it can absorb odors and be stained by some cleaners, especially iodophor. Your best choice for cleaning plastic is percarbonate; use Star San for sanitizing. Sterilizing plastic is not recommended.

Finally, don't get lazy. After you've made a mess in the kitchen on brew day—especially if you've taken Charlie Papazian's advice and had a (few) homebrew(s) while you worked—you might not feel like taking time to clean your equipment. However, leaving the task for later would be a colossal error. Just as it's much easier to rinse a plate covered in spaghetti sauce right after you've eaten and almost impossible to clean it the next morning, your brewing equipment is much easier to clean right after you finish brewing. If you allow your dirty equipment to sit, much of the liquid or runny solids that could have been cleaned up easily will become caked-on crud by the time you get around to washing up.

The correlation between cleanliness and great beer is undeniable, but the reality is that many great beers came about through contamination. Although you probably don't want to experiment with odd microbes growing on your week-old leftover Chinese food, a bit of contamination will not ruin your beer. It won't necessarily give you bad beer, either. The worst that will happen is an off-flavor here or there, or a really awesome brew that you can't replicate because you don't know what got into it. Homebrewing is fun, so don't turn yourself off to it by turning the cleaning process into a tedious chore.

KNOW-HOW/ TECHNIQUES

One of the best things about brewing beer is that experimentation is a natural part of the process. You can generally make substitutions for the specific malt, hops, and yeast called for in the recipes, whether as a matter of taste or as an adjustment when you can't find the exact ingredient listed. If you want results that are close to those of the original recipe, substitute like-for-like (e.g., a 5 percent alpha acid hop for another 5 percent alpha acid hop). Brand names don't matter for the most part, except with some types of yeast. In the majority of ale styles, pretty much any brand of dry ale yeast will do; liquid yeast are a bit trickier because they can be specific to a certain manufacturer. Another caution about yeast substitutions is that they're more difficult to pull off for beer styles

that have an identifiable yeast taste, such as saisons. If you have no choice but to substitute in such a case, do careful research to identify an appropriate substitution.

FULL MASH BREWING

Anyone who can cook oatmeal, grits, polenta, or any grain-based dish on a stovetop can make an all-grain beer. You'll get down to basics and learn how to create wort by mashing (extracting the sugars from the grain in warm water) and lautering (separating the steeped grain from the sweet liquid). Mashing and lautering are both fairly simple three-step processes.

NOTE: Many beer recipe kits come with grains premeasured into a mesh bag and ready to mash; you could also put your grains in your own mesh bag, available from any homebrew supplier. For the most part, however, you can easily work with loose grain, assuming you have a strong arm (and spoon) to circulate your mash. Most important is to make sure the grains don't stick together in a clump so that the wort can't circulate through.

MASHING

Making your mash is one of the easiest things you'll do as a homebrewer. Here's what it takes:

1. Boil water.

2. Turn off the heat. Cool the water to a specific temperature (typically between 165°F and 180°F).

3. Add the grains, and steep. Some recipes call for more steeping than others. While steeping for the specified amount of time, maintain the specified temperature. If your water gets too cool, just warm it back up to temperature. Some homebrewers simmer their grains at a low boil for up to an hour and strain the wort at that point. If you use this technique, you'll get the most from your grains by mashing at a temperature 30°F to 45°F shy of boiling.

LAUTERING

After you let your grains steep for the recommended time, it's time for lautering, or separating the mash from the wort. It's another three-step process, consisting of *mashout, recirculation*, and *sparging*.

1. You may want to start your lautering process by doing a mashout, which effectively turns off the enzymes in your grain. It "freezes" your sugar level and keeps your grains from gumming up, allowing for easy wort draining. If your grains are pretty loose after steeping, you can skip the mashout. However, if your grains are sticky enough to make draining the wort difficult, reheat your mash to about 170°F, either by returning the brew pot to its heat source or by adding hot water (previously boiled and cooled) to your mash. At this stage, your wort may be cloudy with proteins; don't worry, it will become clearer as it cools. If you're seeing bits of grain in the liquid, strain again until clear.

2. This takes you to the next step in lautering: recirculation, the easiest way to remove unwanted debris from your wort. To do this, place a mesh strainer over a second pot and pour your mash through it. Then clear out any debris from the empty pot, move the grain-filled strainer to it, and pour the wort through again. Usually, a couple of passes are all you need to get the grain debris out of your wort. You'll end up with a potful of clean wort and a strainer full of mashed grains.

3. Finally, rinse your grains by sparging. Typically, sparging requires a quantity of clean water equal to about 50 percent of the volume of wort. For the recipes in this book, you'll sparge with a little more than 1 gallon of water. The previously boiled water should still be warm, but not too hot (a maximum of 170°F). To set up for sparging, put the strainer full of grains over the pot of clean wort. Slowly pour (sparging means "to sprinkle") the sparging water through the grains into the wort. Try using a measuring cup or soup ladle to distribute a trickle of water evenly across the surface of the grains. The sparge is a gradual process. It should take you at least 30 minutes to pour all of the sparge water through the grains; with larger batches, you may sparge for an hour or more.

Once you've finished sparging, your grains are "spent" and can be thrown out, used as compost, or donated for animal feed (if you keep chickens, you can give it to them). You also can cook with *spent grain* as a flour substitute when making foods such as bread, pizza dough, pasta, and cookies. To make spent-grain flour, dry the grain in a food dehydrator or on low heat in the oven and grind it in a food processor or spice grinder until it's the consistency of flour. Spent grain freezes well.

YEAST PITCHING AND FERMENTATION

A common joke is that people don't make beer; yeast make beer. While the action of pitching yeast is simple (i.e., open and pour), you can end up with something that's not quite beer if your yeast isn't pitched at the right temperature or in the correct amount for your batch. Remember that a byproduct of yeast is alcohol. If your beer is faintly alcoholic or nonalcoholic, chances are overwhelming that something went wrong with your yeast.

Yeast are alive and, like all living things, need to be fed and nurtured in order to thrive. Although the New Brew Amber Ale recipe in chapter 1 requires minimal intervention, if you pitched the yeast at the wrong temperature (typically too hot) or if your yeast were already nonfunctional or very weak to begin with, the resulting *attenuation* was doomed from the start. Additionally, if you didn't aerate the wort sufficiently, even healthy yeast could have suffocated.

Yeast are pitched at the end of the cooling process because high temperatures will kill them. However, if the temperature of the wort in your fermentation container is too cool, the yeast will simply go dormant. The good news is that cold yeast aren't dead, so find a warmer storage place and fermentation will resume.

It's crucial to monitor the temperature both outside and inside your fermenter to forestall a possible yeast issue. You may also monitor the fermenting wort with a your hydrometer, and if ABV seems low and you suspect fermentation isn't taking hold, you can and should pitch some more yeast.

You can also make and keep your own yeast starter so as to be sure you're only brewing with the freshest yeast possible.

HOW TO MAKE A YEAST STARTER

Although liquid yeast can be pitched directly into your fermenter, for the best results, make a yeast starter, which is quite easy to do. Why use a starter for liquid yeast? In the recent past, the concentration of yeast cells in liquid yeast strains wasn't great enough to support fermentation. A starter increases the concentration of yeast cells to the point where a packet of yeast packs a respectable fermentation punch. Today, most liquid yeast created for homebrewing contain a sufficient concentration—literally billions of cells—to make yeast starter unnecessary, but it's a good idea to know how to make a starter anyway. It could come in handy if you want to make more beers from the same yeast strain, even if you decide to stick with dry yeast or pitch liquid yeast without a starter.

YEAST STARTER

MAKES 2 CUPS

There are two things to keep in mind when you plan to make a yeast starter: First, yeast needs to be kept in a cool place such as a refrigerator until you're ready to use it; this will keep the cells dormant and healthy. If you mistakenly leave your yeast out and it starts to activate, don't throw it away. Put it in a cool environment to go "back to sleep." Also, use good sanitation practices when making your yeast starter so as not to add contaminants that will interfere with the flavor profile of the yeast.

1 (50-milliliter) packet liquid yeast
2 cups premade wort or ½ cup pale *Dry Malt Extract (DME)*

1. Two to four days before brew day, take the liquid yeast out of the refrigerator and let it warm to room temperature. If it's in a packet that contains a yeast nutrient, activate it by pressing the packet against a flat surface with the heel of your palm. Shake or smack the packet (brewers call these "smack packs") and place it, unopened, in a warm place (about 80°F; try on top of your refrigerator or near a water heater). It will swell. Don't worry if the packet looks like it might burst; this is normal. When the package stops swelling, the yeast are ready to pitch.

2. If using premade wort: In a small saucepan over high heat, bring the wort to a boil. If using DME: In a small saucepan, mix the DME with 2 cups of water and bring it to a boil. Boil the solution for at least 10 minutes. Remove the saucepan from the heat.

3. Set the saucepan in an ice bath or very cold water and quickly cool the starter liquid to the recommended pitching temperature (aim for your fermentation temperature, but no higher than 80°F).

4. Transfer the cooled wort to a medium-size (½-gallon) sanitized screw-top bottle and screw on the sanitized lid.

5. Sanitize the outside of the liquid yeast packet before opening it. Sanitize any utensil (e.g., scissors) you'll use to open the packet.

6. Open the packet and the bottle and pitch the liquid yeast into the wort. Close the bottle and shake it vigorously to aerate the wort.

7. Replace the bottle's lid with a sanitized stopper fitted with an airlock. Alternatively, you can top the bottle loosely with sanitized aluminum foil or plastic wrap, securely enough to protect the starter from contaminants but gently enough to allow carbon dioxide to escape. The starter will begin fizzing as the yeast begin to multiply.

8. Place the starter in a warm, dry area where you can monitor it. Shake it lightly every couple of hours.

9. After a day or so, the yeast should start settling to the bottom of the jar. At this point, you can either add more boiled and cooled starter wort to grow more yeast, or you can pitch the starter into your beer fermenter as you would rehydrated dry yeast.

SERVING AND DRINKING

Believe it or not, beer should be served from a glass, the popularity of Red Solo cups notwithstanding. Fortunately, modern manufacturers are making a variety of glasses designed for specific beer styles. One of the pioneers in promoting dedicated glassware for beer is none other than Boston Beer Company's Jim Koch. For years, he has understood that to enjoy a beer to its fullest, you need to savor it.

The following types of glassware are typically used to serve craft beer (including the optimal temperature range):

Flute   IPA   Mug (stein)

Goblet   Lager

FLUTE Best with wild beers or highly carbonated brews. As Champagne has proven, this style of glass enhances effervescence. *(46–48°F)*

GOBLET Good for higher ABV beers and brews with strong aromas; great at head retention for Tripels and Quads. *(50–55°F)*

IPA The first Spiegelau beer glass. After initially refusing to meet with Jim Koch to design the perfect lager vessel, famed glass maker Spiegelau saw the error of its ways and began to seek out some of the nation's best beer makers to design perfect glasses for their beer. The first in their effort was this IPA glass, which was a collaboration with Sam Calagione of Dogfish Head and Ken Grossman of Sierra Nevada. The glass has a narrow, rippled base and a tulip-style top that maximizes head retention and accentuates hops aroma. *(45–50°F)*

LAGER A thin-walled glass designed to enhance clarity of the beer. The glass tends to be tall, with minimal curvature as it goes up. Best for non-pilsner lager brews.*(35–48°F)*

MUG (STEIN) The quintessential beer garden vessel; best for large quantities of easy-drinking, low-ABV lager beer. *(35–48°F)*

PILSNER A tall, slender, tapered glass ideally suited for clear, effervescent lager beer. *(46–48°F)*

PINT (CONICAL) Common more because it's cheap and easy to produce rather than because it does much for beer flavor. This is the ubiquitous conical tumbler in which bars across America serve draft beer (as well as many other beverages). A true pint glass holds 16 ounces, but many bars sell "pints" in tumblers that actually hold 12 ounces. (Next time you order a standard 12-ounce bottle, ask for a pint glass and pour in the beer. Unless you're at a bar that takes its beer very seriously, the "pint" glass will be full.) As Americans become increasingly

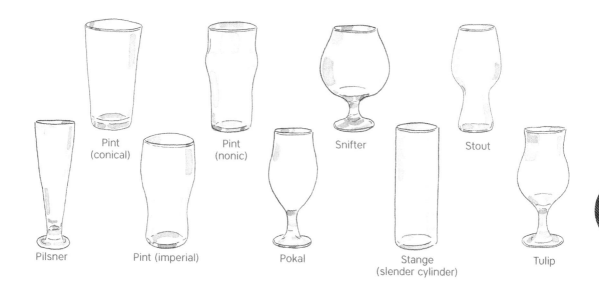

Pilsner
Pint (conical)
Pint (imperial)
Pint (nonic)
Pokal
Snifter
Stange (slender cylinder)
Stout
Tulip

sophisticated about beer, more and more bars are getting away from this style. *(40–55° F)*

PINT (IMPERIAL)   A 20-ounce version of the conical pint typically used in Britain. Great with Extra Special Bitters brews. *(40–55°F)*

PINT (NONIC)   A pint designed for ease of storage and to reduce breakage. The slight bulge at the rim of the glass reduces chips and adds a grip, leading to fewer dropped glasses. Available in both American (16 ounce) and British (imperial) versions. *(40–55°F)*

POKAL   Slightly more elegant than a pilsner glass and more refined than a pint. This glass is often called the "European Pilsner" glass and is notable for its small stem and large foot. Like the pilsner, it's designed for light, bubbly lagers. *(46–48°F)*

SNIFTER   More familiar as a vessel for cognac or brandy, but often used for high-ABV, aromatic beers that improve as they warm (e.g., Russian Imperial Stout, Barleywine). *(50–70°F)*

STANGE (SLENDER CYLINDER)   Another glass type typically found in Germany. This tall, straight-sided glass is perfect for malt-forward beers, along with some fruit beers. *(40–50°F)*

STOUT   Another collaboration beer glass made by Spiegelau and the brewers at Left Hand Brewing Company and Rogue Ales. Its appearance is very similar to the IPA glass, with a narrow, cylindrical base that rises to a smooth, tulip-shaped bulb. *(55°F, British Cellar Temperature)*

TULIP   A great glass for beers with abundant head retention; often used for double IPAs and Strong Ales. It has a bulbous base with a short stem, similar to a "shortened" wine glass. *(50–70°F)*

Wheat

Weizen

Wine

WEIZEN Another proprietary glass, this time from the Bavaria region of Germany, where the beer originates. With thin walls and a long flute, the glass showcases the beer's color and maximizes the good head retention associated with weizen beers. The shape of this glass also perfectly targets the banana-phenol aromas common in this style. *(48–54°F)*

WHEAT Another Spiegelau entry made with Larry Bell of Bell's Brewing. The glass has a short, stout stem beneath a voluminous bowl that aims to retain the nuanced aromas of wheat beer. *(40–50°F)*

WINE The familiar "red wine" shape. Many retailers are replacing pint glasses with wine glasses, both for presentation and for economy; wine glasses can easily replace goblets, tulips, and even snifters for beer pours. *(varies depending on the more traditional glass it is replacing)*

When it comes to pouring beer, you want to consider how much head there should be on a beer. Believe it or not, there are beer-pouring competitions that bring bartenders from around the world together to "pour off" before a panel of judges.

Here are the steps to pouring a perfect beer:

1. Rinse the glass. Any soap or other residue on the inside of your glass—even if it's clean—can affect head retention.

2. Pour at an angle to start. You want the beer to pour smoothly, so limit the distance between the source of your beer and the base of your glass by allowing the beer to flow down the side of the glass; try to do this without touching the edge of the glass with the can, bottle, or tap line.

3. As you pour, level the glass and move the stream away from the side, keeping in mind how much head you want to retain. Pouring closer to the glass will create less foam than will pouring farther away; always pour to the center of the glass once it is level.

4. If pouring from a bottle or can, leave about ¼ inch of beer in its bottom. Most beer has sediment; your homebrew certainly will. You don't want to create cloudy beer from that last bit of brew. This is another reason why pouring into a glass is better than drinking from the bottle or can: Any sediment will remain at the bottom of the container rather than being jostled into the beer from multiple sips.

MASTER TIPS

Water is probably the ingredient most US homebrewers take for granted, but you shouldn't. You're probably used to the idea that if you have access to a municipal water supply, you may never second-guess your water until there's a natural disaster that forces you into the grocery store to stock up on the bottled stuff. Even the majority of bottled water in the United States comes from municipal sources. But the water coming out of your tap may be treated with chlorine and/or fluoride, and it may contain other minerals that are difficult to eradicate. What's in your water will probably end up in your beer. Boiling the water first, as you do when brewing, will eliminate some (but not all) of the chemicals in city water, but sometimes it intensifies the undesirable chemicals. Using tap water means you'll incorporate substances into your beer that you don't want in the recipe.

One of the reasons different regions of the world produce different styles of beer is that, until recently, brewers had to rely on whatever water flowed within easy distance of their breweries. There were no shipments of mineral water bottled in the Alps, and there were no breweries with their own large-scale water purification equipment. As much as craft beer drinkers are apt to disparage mass-market beers like Miller, those beers succeeded as much by guaranteeing consistent water quality as by effective marketing.

Most brewers do a water analysis before launching a brand or moving to a new location. For example, when brewer Matt Barbee of Rockmill Brewery in Lancaster, Ohio, discovered that his local water was almost identical to that in Waldonia, Belgium, he decided to focus on brewing Belgian farmhouse beers.

But you don't have to jump through these hoops to make great beer. Just make sure your water's as free of impurities as you can make it. At a minimum, it's a good idea to run your water through a standard carbon filter before using it, even if you like the taste of your water straight from the tap. You can buy a basic pitcher model or tap hookup at any housewares store. This kind of filter will partially remove some basic impurities, such as lead, chlorine, pesticides, and industrial pollutants. If you want to go a step further, you can brew with distilled water mineralized with a dash of kosher salt. Never brew with hard water, such as that from a non-municipal water source like a well, lake, or cistern.

4

CRAFT BEER RECIPES

In this section, there are five classic beer recipes that you can make from scratch: a pale ale recipe that shows you how to make mash from grain; a creamy porter recipe that demonstrates how to pitch with liquid yeast; a Berliner Weisse recipe that gives you a shot at making sour beer; an American IPA recipe that yields a beer most craft brewers think of as the quintessential American brew; and a pilsner recipe that introduces you to lager. Making the recipes will give you a solid foundation in most brewing styles, along with pointers on challenges such as all-grain brewing, making a starter for liquid yeast, and making a sour mash. Even if they're unfamiliar at first, all the ingredients are readily available through homebrewing stores and websites. After brewing these five beers, you should be able to tackle any beer recipe with confidence.

4

A PROPER MASH: ALL-GRAIN PALE ALE

The New Brew Amber Ale recipe in Chapter 1 used LME, but many homebrewing recipes are based on all-grain or partial mash techniques. For your first foray into grain, you'll go the full barley, creating your first mash. The following table explains what to look for when you make all-grain pale ale.

ALL-GRAIN PALE ALE CHARACTERISTICS	
Gravity	OG = 1.050; FG = 1.012
ABV	5.5%
Appearance	Pale golden to deep amber in color; moderately large, white head with solid retention.
Flavor	Fairly high bitterness balanced by the biscuit-like flavor of the specialty malts; low caramel tones.
Aroma	Moderate hop aroma with citrusy characteristics; low maltiness with possible bready tones; low fruit *esters*.
Mouthfeel	Moderately dry finish; moderately high carbonation. Very smooth with little to no astringency.
Aftertaste	The hops and malt flavors can linger.
Overall Impression	Very well balanced despite the high hop profile.

ALL-GRAIN PALE ALE

MAKES 2½ GALLONS

This recipe is for a straightforward American-style pale ale, so you can focus on learning how to create the wort by mashing and lautering grain. American Pale Ale typically uses all-American hops for a bitter but balanced beer.

4 pounds American 2-row pale malt

1½ pounds German Vienna malt

½ pound wheat malt

¼ pound Special B Belgian malt

½ ounce Amarillo hops (7% alpha acid)

¼ ounce Cascade hops (6.6% alpha acid)

¼ ounce Magnum hops (14.5% alpha acid)

½ (11.5-gram/0.405-ounce) package ale yeast, such as Safale US-05

⅓ cup corn sugar for priming bottles

1. In a 5-gallon brew pot over high heat, bring 2 gallons of water to a boil. Remove the brew pot from the heat. Transfer 2 cups of the water to a sanitized glass jar; set it aside to cool. Allow the water in the brew pot to cool to about 160°F.

2. Steep the American, German Vienna, wheat, and Belgian malts in the water for 40 minutes, maintaining a temperature of 160°F. If you need to reheat the mash, do not exceed that temperature.

3. Lauter per the instructions on page 50. The wort should end up in the brew pot.

4. Bring the wort to a rolling boil per the instructions on page 18.

5. Add the Amarillo and Cascade hops and boil for 55 minutes.

6. Add the Magnum hops and boil for an additional 5 minutes.

7. In a separate, clean saucepan, bring 1 gallon of water to a boil. Remove from the heat and allow the water to cool to room temperature; set aside.

8. Remove the brew pot from the heat. From this point on, make sure everything that comes into contact with the wort has been sanitized.

9. Cool the wort quickly; it should take no longer than 30 minutes for the wort to cool to below 80°F. Do not slow-chill the wort. Chill using one of two methods: Either (1) transfer the entire brew pot to a very icy bath (the kitchen sink, a bathtub, or a large cooler is good for holding an ice bath) or (2) place an immersion chiller in the wort.

10. While the wort is chilling, check the temperature of the 2 cups of reserved boiled water; it should be between 95°F and 100°F. Do not add unsanitized water to cool or warm the reserved water: If necessary, reheat it or set it aside to cool further. Rehydrate the yeast by sprinkling it on top of the warm water and allowing it to dissolve. Loosely cover the jar with plastic wrap and set it aside for about 15 minutes, then gently swirl the solution.

11. Filter out the hops debris by pouring the chilled wort through a sanitized strainer into a sanitized 3-gallon fermenting container. Alternatively, whirlpool the wort and siphon it into the fermenter.

Continued

12. Add the boiled, cooled water from step 7 to the fermenting container to bring the total amount of wort to 2½ gallons. Shake the fermenter vigorously or pour the wort back and forth between the fermenter and brew pot to aerate it.

13. When the temperature of the wort is less than 80°F, pitch the yeast. Cover the fermenter. Plug it with an airlock containing sanitizer or a blowoff hose (which doesn't clog as easily) that flows into a jar of water. If using the hose, replace it with an airlock after the lively primary fermentation dies down in a couple of days.

14. Ferment the beer at 68°F to 73°F for 2 weeks. Regularly check the temperatures shown on the fermenter thermometer and a room thermometer; maintain a stable temperature wherever you're fermenting.

15. If you're doing a *secondary fermentation* (see below), rack the beer into the second fermenter after 5 days.

16. After fermenting for a total of about 2 weeks (the temperature of the beer should hold steady for three consecutive days), bottle the beer (per the instructions on page 20), and allow it to condition for 2 to 4 weeks.

SECONDARY FERMENTATION

The main reason brewers ferment their beers more than once, with a secondary or even tertiary fermentation, is to give it greater clarity and a cleaner taste. When beer ferments, dead yeast settles to the bottom of the fermenter. You want to leave that trub behind when you siphon off the beer, whether into bottles or into a second fermenter. However, even after siphoning, your beer will still have plenty of sediment, which might give it a pronounced yeasty taste. If that's the case, a secondary fermentation will most likely improve its flavor. When you rack your beer to another fermenter, secondary fermentation will make even more yeast sediment settle out. The beer clarifies and becomes purer and tastier. A secondary fermentation is not necessary for most ales, and is typically employed only when you have a high original gravity necessitating a longer fermentation process.

When first starting out on your homebrewing adventure, you probably won't want to take the extra time for this step—it'll postpone the moment you finally get to drink your beer. But if you want to find out what secondary fermentation is all about, go for it. All you'll need is a second carboy. The steps are simple:

1. Make sure all equipment has been thoroughly sanitized.

2. Syphon the wort into the secondary container, using care to leave the trub in the bottom of the primary fermentation vessel.

3. Take a hydrometer reading; if fermentation is slow, repitch your yeast (you can use standard brewer's yeast at this stage).

THROUGH A GLASS DARKLY: TRADITIONAL ENGLISH PORTER

For this recipe, you'll try another something new: pitching liquid yeast. Dry yeast are less expensive and easier to use, but the many more strains of liquid yeast can produce some really intriguing results that add variety to your homebrewing. If you're making a basic pale ale, there's no reason not to use dry yeast; they generally do their job without much tending. However, ale yeast are pretty much for making pale ales, and the further from pale ale the beer style you're going for is, the less likely it is that dry yeast will yield an accurate example of that style. Will it still taste good? Of course, but it won't hit the same flavor marks as beer made with yeast harvested specifically for that style. That's why this porter recipe calls for liquid yeast. When you get around to brewing saisons and weizens (and all the Belgians, for that matter), you'll also want to use liquid yeast. The following table explains what to look for when you make a porter.

PORTER CHARACTERISTICS	
Gravity	OG = 1.055; FG = 1.014
ABV	5.5%
Appearance	Ruby brown to deep brown in color, approaching black; should have some clarity when held up to a light source. Head is creamy brown with good retention.
Flavor	Strong malt profile with a slight burnt finish; moderately high bitterness owing to the hops, which balance the malts nicely.
Aroma	Strong roasted malt, occasional burnt or smoky aromas; caramel, toffee, coffee, and bready aromas are often present. Very few esters, but hops are agreeably present. No fruity tones.
Mouthfeel	Medium-sweet finish, somewhat astringent character. Moderate carbonation. Thick and creamy.
Aftertaste	Chocolate, coffee, or burnt flavors may linger; hop bitterness shouldn't be overpowering.
Overall Impression	Complex, flavorful, roasty.

4

TRADITIONAL ENGLISH PORTER

MAKES 2½ GALLONS

This recipe makes a more-or-less traditional porter (remember, porters have a very eclectic history, the recipe having been changed every generation or so for 300 years). Made with both a mash and an LME, it brews a little easier than an all-grain recipe; the pale LME enhances the flavor and moderates the beer's roasty intensity. The liquid Irish ale yeast from White Labs, a fermentation science lab in San Diego, California, is perfect for this darker brew and for beers with a higher specific gravity. If you decide to use the More Powerful Porter recipe variation (see page 66), which adds more sugar to the boil, the yeast will do a superb job.

¼ pound Victory malt

¼ pound wheat malt

¼ pound chocolate malt

¼ pound Bairds British Crystal malt (70/80°L)

4 pounds Alexander's Pale LME

½ ounce Chinook hops (13% alpha acid)

¼ teaspoon Irish moss

½ ounce Cascade hops (5.5% alpha acid)

½ pound invert sugar (see page 66), optional

½ ounce French Strisselspalt hops
(3.5% alpha acid)

1 vial Wyeast 1084 liquid Irish Ale yeast

⅓ cup corn sugar for priming bottles

1. In a 5-gallon brew pot over high heat, bring 3 gallons of water to a boil. Remove the brew pot from the heat. Allow the water in the brew pot to cool to about 180°F.

2. Steep the Victory, wheat, chocolate, and crystal malts in the water for 20 minutes, maintaining a temperature of 180°F. If you need to reheat the mash, do not exceed that temperature.

3. Lauter per the instructions on page 50. The wort should end up in the brew pot. If necessary, return the wort to the stove and heat at medium until the temperature is about 165°F.

4. Stir in the LME. Be sure to dissolve it thoroughly, so the beer doesn't end up completely opaque.

5. Bring the wort to a rolling boil per the instructions on page 18.

6. Add the Chinook hops and boil for 40 minutes.

7. Add the Irish moss and boil for 10 minutes.

8. Add the Cascade hops and boil for 8 minutes.

9. If making More Powerful Porter, add the invert sugar and boil for 3 minutes.

10. Add the French Strisselspalt hops and boil for 2 minutes.

11. In a separate, clean saucepan, bring 1 gallon of water to a boil. Remove from the heat and allow the water to cool to room temperature. Set aside.

12. From this point on, make sure everything that comes into contact with the wort has been sanitized.

13. Cool the wort quickly per the instructions on page 61.

14. Filter out the hops debris per the instructions on page 61.

15. Add the boiled, cooled water from step 11 to the fermenting container to bring the total amount of wort to 2½ gallons. Aerate the wort per the instructions on page 19.

16. When the temperature of the wort is less than 80°F, pitch the liquid yeast. Although you can pitch this yeast into the wort as is, per the instructions on the package, you'll get better results if you make a yeast starter (see page 52). You'll need to begin the process of making the starter at least 2 days—and up to a week—before you brew.

17. Ferment per the instructions on page 19, maintaining a temperature between 65°F and 75°F. Don't worry if it takes a bit longer for fermentation to become noticeable than it does with other beers: So long as the temperature is within range, it may take up to 5 days for significant bubbling to appear in the airlock or through the blowoff hose.

18. Ferment for a total of 2 to 3 weeks per the instructions on page 19. If you wish, do a secondary fermentation per the instructions on page 62.

19. Bottle and condition the beer per the instructions on page 20.

VARIATION: MORE POWERFUL PORTER

To make a porter with a higher ABV, you can add ½ pound of invert sugar to the wort 55 minutes into the boil (i.e., your boil time with sugar = 5 minutes). Invert sugar is best used in porters, but you can try adding it to other recipes to intensify their caramel flavors.

INVERT SUGAR

MAKES 2 POUNDS (ABOUT 1 QUART)

Invert sugar has a long shelf life. You can store it in an airtight container in your refrigerator for up to 6 months.

4¼ cups extra-fine granulated sugar
¼ teaspoon cream of tartar

1. In a medium saucepan, combine the sugar and the cream of tartar with 2 cups of water. Cook over medium-high heat, stirring gently, until the mixture comes to a boil. Once the mixture is boiling, use a wet spoon or pastry brush to remove any sugar crystals stuck to the side of the saucepan.

2. Reduce the heat to prevent boil-over, and insert a candy thermometer. Continue boiling, without stirring, until the mixture reaches 236°F.

3. Remove the saucepan from the heat and cover. Let the sugar cool to room temperature. The texture should be roughly that of liquid corn syrup.

CREATING SOUR BEER: SPRINGTIME IN BERLIN(ER WEISSE)

Beginning brewers are typically warned: Don't try to make a sour beer. Nonetheless, sour beers are wonderful to brew, and even a new home-brewer can tackle this particular recipe, which begins by teaching you how to make a sour mash. The beer you'll be making is a Berliner Weisse, a sessionable beer named for its city of origin. Referred to as "the Champagne of the north" by Napoleon's troops, this beer is just as highly regulated. Where Champagne-style wine must be made in Champagne to bear the name Champagne, so must beers in the Berliner Weisse style be made in Berlin to properly be called Berliner Weisse. Since you're homebrewing, you can simply call it a perfectly refreshing summertime brew. Professor Fritz Briem 1809 and Southampton Berliner Weisse are good examples of the style. The following table explains what to look for when you make a Berliner Weisse.

BERLINER WEISSE CHARACTERISTICS	
Gravity	OG = 1.030; FG = 1.004
ABV	4.5%
Appearance	Pale straw in color; often hazy; dense white head with little to no retention. Effervescent.
Flavor	Lactic sourness is the predominant flavor; not too acidic. Bread or wheat qualities, with no hop flavors or off-flavor *DMS*. Fruity or Brettanomyces flavors may be present depending on what kind of bacteria grew during mashing.
Aroma	Sharply sour, even acidic. Fruitiness that can smell flowery as the beer ages. Zero hop aroma. Commercial varieties will have a mild Brettanomyces aroma; homebrew may or may not have a Brettanomyces presence depending on environmental conditions.
Mouthfeel	Very well carbonated with fine bubbles. Light body and dry finish. No alcohol notes.
Aftertaste	Tartness can linger.
Overall Impression	Very refreshing with low ABV.

SPRINGTIME IN BERLIN(ER WEISSE)

This Berliner Weisse is a traditional sour, tart, and effervescent ale with a slightly higher ABV than you would traditionally find in Berlin (where Berliner Weisse typically has less than 3 percent ABV). This is a great beer for hot summer days, and you can experiment by adding flavored (e.g., raspberry or cassis) syrups to the brew during bottling.

3 pounds German Pilsner malt, divided
2½ pounds German wheat malt
½ ounce Hallertauer hops (4% alpha acid)
½ (11.5-gram/0.405-ounce) package ale yeast, such as Safale US-05
⅓ cup corn sugar for priming bottles

1. Three days prior to brewing, bring 2½ cups of water to a boil in a saucepan over high heat. Remove from the heat and cool to 130°F.

2. Add ½ pound of the German Pilsner malt, stirring gently.

3. When the temperature of the wort reaches 120°F, cover the pan with a lid and steep the grain for 45 minutes. Monitor the temperature continuously and return the saucepan to the heat as needed to maintain a steady temperature.

4. Remove the lid and cover the saucepan with plastic wrap so that no air can get in. Place the saucepan in a warm (ideally 115°F), dry location for 3 days; a closed gas oven will typically be this warm, or choose a spot near a radiator or water heater. Check the temperature periodically. This will be the sour mash.

5. On brew day, bring 3 gallons of water to a boil in a 5-gallon brew pot. Remove the brew pot from the heat. Transfer 2 cups of the water to a sanitized glass jar and set it aside to cool. Allow the water in the brew pot to cool to 160°F.

6. Steep the remaining 2½ pounds Pilsner malt and the 2½ pounds wheat malt in the brew pot for 40 minutes, maintaining a temperature of 149°F to 155°F. Stir gently. If you need to reheat the mash, do not exceed that temperature range.

7. Add the sour mash, stirring gently until circulated.

8. Lauter per the instructions on page 50, doing the mashout at 170°F. The wort should end up in the brew pot.

9. Bring the wort to a rolling boil per the instructions on page 18. Boil for 30 minutes.

10. Add the hops and boil for 15 minutes.

11. In a separate, clean saucepan, bring 1 gallon of water to a boil. Remove from the heat and allow the water to cool to room temperature. Set aside.

12. Remove the brew pot from the heat. From this point on, make sure everything that comes into contact with the wort has been sanitized.

13. Cool the wort quickly per the instructions on page 61.

14. While the wort is chilling, rehydrate the yeast per the instructions on page 19.

15. Filter out the hops debris and transfer the chilled wort to a sanitized 3-gallon fermenting container per the instructions on page 61.

16. Add the boiled, cooled water from step 11 to the fermenting container to bring the total amount of wort to 2½ gallons, and aerate per the instructions on page 19.

17. When the temperature of the wort is less than 80°F, pitch the yeast.

18. Ferment for 2 weeks per the instructions on page 19, maintaining a temperature of 75°F.

19. Bottle and condition the beer per the instructions on page 20.

GETTING BITTER WITH IT: HOP-A-PALOOZA LEFTOVER HOPS IPA

Now that you've brewed a few beers, you may have a collection of leftover hops that you'd like to use up. Hops store well in an airtight container in a cool place (for long-term hops storage, use your freezer), but they're like cooking spices: The longer you wait to use them, the less potent they are. When you find yourself with a quarter ounce of this and a quarter ounce of that, it's time to pull out this recipe and use up your leftover hops. Six-hop beer recipes are popular, and "hopheads" line up for niche beers on a regular basis. For instance, Heady Topper, a double IPA brewed by The Alchemist, is one of the most sought-after beers in the United States. So many out-of-state cars were pulling into the Waterbury, Vermont, brewery that the brewers decided to close the facility to visitors. More readily available examples of the style include Lagunitas IPA, Bear Republic Racer 5 IPA, Dogfish Head 60-Minute IPA (and 90-Minute, a higher-ABV double IPA), and Stone IPA (and Stone's "Enjoy By" double IPA series). You no longer have to worry that the keg of exquisite IPA you're craving might be empty five minutes after it's tapped at your favorite bar. Now you have the tools and recipe for making your own six-hop IPA. You can "enjoy by" yourself whenever you want. The following table explains what to look for when you make an American-style IPA.

AMERICAN-STYLE IPA CHARACTERISTICS	
Gravity	OG = 1.070; FG = 1.016
ABV	6.5% to 7.5% for this recipe (double IPAs range from 7.5% to 10%)
Appearance	Deep gold to deep amber in color; clear with good head retention. Unfiltered (i.e., dry hopped) versions can be a bit hazy.
Flavor	High hop character with citrus, floral, and pine notes. Clean malt with a bit of caramel or toast flavor. Low fruit qualities.
Aroma	Intense, almost perfume-like hop aromas of citrus, pine, fruit, and resins. Slight alcohol smell, especially in a double IPA, is acceptable.
Mouthfeel	Slight astringency with a dry finish. Moderate carbonation. Some warming qualities are acceptable at the higher range of ABV and are to be expected in a double IPA. Slight body, especially as compared with its English or Belgian counterparts.
Aftertaste	Bitterness tends to linger but should not leave a harsh aftertaste.
Overall Impression	It's all about the hops; without a strong bitter profile, it wouldn't be an IPA.

HOP-A-PALOOZA LEFTOVER HOPS IPA

MAKES 2½ GALLONS

One rule of thumb in brewing is that the longer the boil, the more bitter the brew. In this recipe, you'll boil for 90 minutes instead of the 60 minutes called for in this book's other recipes. You can use whatever hops you like to experiment with this recipe, but you should try to match alpha acid percentages given here with any hops substitution.

3½ pounds American 2-row pale malt

1 pound German Vienna malt

¼ pound Caramel malt (20°L)

1 ounce Simcoe hops (13% alpha acid)

½ ounce Columbus hops (14.5% alpha acid)

¼ ounce Apollo hops (18% alpha acid)

½ ounce Citra hops (13.2% alpha acid; whole flower preferred)

¼ ounce Amarillo hops (9.5% alpha acid)

¼ ounce Cascade hops (6.6% alpha acid)

½ (11.5-gram/0.405-ounce) package ale yeast, such as Safale US-05

½ ounce Columbus hops (optional; 15% alpha acid; whole flower preferred; for pellets, use a mesh bag)

½ ounce Centennial hops (10% alpha acid; whole flower preferred; for pellets, use a mesh bag)

⅓ cup corn sugar for priming bottles

1. Over high heat, bring 3 gallons of water to a boil in a 5-gallon brew pot. Remove the brew pot from the heat. Transfer 2 cups of the water to a sanitized glass jar and set it aside to cool. Allow the water in the brew pot to cool to 160°F.

2. Steep the pale, German Vienna, and Caramel malts in the water for 60 minutes, maintaining a temperature of 145°F. As this is a very long steep, monitor the temperature especially carefully. If you need to reheat the mash, do not exceed 145°F.

3. Lauter per the instructions on page 50. The wort should end up in the brew pot.

4. Bring the wort to a rolling boil per the instructions on page 18.

5. Add the Simcoe, Columbus, and Apollo hops and boil for 45 minutes.

6. Add the Citra, Amarillo, and Cascade hops and boil for another 45 minutes.

7. In a separate, clean saucepan, bring 1 gallon of water to a boil. Remove from the heat and allow the water to cool to room temperature. Set aside.

8. Remove the brew pot from the heat. From this point on, make sure everything that comes into contact with the wort has been sanitized.

Continued

9. Cool the wort quickly per the instructions on page 61.

10. While the wort is chilling, rehydrate the yeast per the instructions on page 19.

11. Filter out the hops debris and transfer the chilled wort to a sanitized 3-gallon fermenting container per the instructions on page 61.

12. Add the boiled, cooled water from step 7 to the fermenter to bring the total amount of wort to 2½ gallons, and aerate per the instructions on page 19.

13. When the temperature is less than 80°F, pitch the yeast.

14. If you're dry hopping, add the Columbus hops to your fermenter.

15. Ferment for 5 days per the instructions on page 19, maintaining a temperature of 68°F.

16. Do a secondary fermentation per the instructions on page 61.

17. If you're dry hopping, add the Centennial hops.

18. Ferment at 70°F to 72°F for another week to 10 days.

19. Bottle and condition the beer per the instructions on page 20.

COOLING DOWN WITH A LAGER: PRISTINE PILSNER

Up to now, you've brewed only ales. The two main reasons homebrewers tend to shy away from lager brewing are time and temperature. Unless you have a dedicated refrigerator for fermenting your beer, you'll have to store your fermenting lager next to your milk and orange juice for the better part of two months. Two months? That's right, lager takes a lot longer to ferment than ale does. You need patience to brew lager. The following table explains what to look for when you make a pilsner.

PILSNER CHARACTERISTICS	
Gravity	OG = 1.050; FG=1.010
ABV	4.5% to 6%
Appearance	Straw to pale gold in color; good head; clear and bright.
Flavor	Medium-to-high hop bitterness; moderately high malt profile.
Aroma	Malty (not fruity) with moderate hop aroma; slight DMS flavor okay.
Mouthfeel	Creamy, rich, and well carbonated.
Aftertaste	None.
Overall Impression	Refreshing, with stronger malt and hops profile than a classic American lager beer.

CRAFT BEER RECIPES

PRISTINE PILSNER

MAKES 2½ GALLONS

Once you taste this very simple, crisp lager, you'll no doubt want to make more. The recipe is based on a classic European pilsner and uses both a grain mash and liquid yeast. Although many American pilsners use *adjuncts* (especially corn) to add sweetness, this recipe relies on malt to yield a very balanced beer.

1 package Wyeast 2007 pilsen lager liquid yeast; more if needed

4 pounds German pilsner malt

¼ pound Carapils malt (may substitute Caramalt)

1 ounce Hallertauer hops (4% alpha acid)

1 teaspoon Irish moss

⅓ cup corn sugar for priming bottles

1. Several days before you're going to brew, begin a yeast starter per the instructions on page 52.

2. On brew day, bring 3 gallons of water to a boil in a 5-gallon brew pot. Remove the brew pot from the heat. Allow the water in the brew pot to cool to 155°F.

3. Add the malts and steep for 20 minutes, maintaining a temperature of at least 145°F. If you need to reheat the mash, do not exceed that temperature.

4. Lauter per the instructions on page 50. The wort should end up in the brew pot.

5. Bring the wort to a rolling boil per the instructions on page 18.

6. Add the hops and boil for 50 minutes.

7. Add the Irish moss and boil for 10 minutes.

8. In a separate, clean saucepan, bring 1 gallon of water to a boil. Remove from the heat and allow the water to cool to room temperature. Set aside.

9. Remove the brew pot from the heat. From this point on, make sure everything that comes into contact with the wort has been sanitized.

10. Cool the wort quickly per the instructions on page 61.

11. Filter out the hops debris and transfer the chilled wort to a sanitized 3-gallon fermenting container per the instructions on page 61.

12. Add the boiled, cooled water from step 8 to the fermenter to bring the total amount of wort to 2½ gallons, and aerate per the instructions on page 19.

13. When the temperature is about 55°F, pitch the liquid yeast starter.

14. Ferment for 2 weeks at 48°F to 56°F. Like ale yeast, lager yeast won't perform well outside the proper temperature range. Chances are, your refrigerator is colder than this, so monitoring the temperature inside the fermenter and inside the refrigerator is important. If your refrigerator is too cold, wrap the fermenter in some form of insulation, such as a towel.

15. After 2 weeks, do a secondary fermentation per the instructions on page 61. Store the fermenter at 40°F. You're now *lagering* the beer, which will take about 6 weeks.

16. Bottle the beer per the instructions on page 20. If your lager is very clear to the point of being watery, try repitching some yeast. If you do so, pitch it into the sugar priming solution at room temperature. Make sure to use the same strain you used during brewing; you'll need only about ¼ cup of yeast starter (or you can use dry lager yeast if you're desperate). Do not overpitch, as the buildup of carbonation can cause *bottle bombs*.

17. Condition the bottles for 2 to 4 weeks.

18. Chill your lager thoroughly before serving.

CRAFT BEER RECIPES

5

GETTING CREATIVE

For most commercial craft brewers, producing beer isn't about the awards or accolades they may receive in brewing competitions, and it's certainly not about making money or becoming famous. It's about the beer. Sure, brewers love what they do, and everyone needs a pat on the back—or a gold medal at the Great American Beer Festival— now and again. However, the main reason craft beer exists today is because a bunch of homebrewers absolutely loved beer and couldn't stand what was happening to the US beer industry in the middle of the 20th century. Americans were drinking mass-produced suds that many beer lovers considered swill, and were entirely missing the point of beer, as homebrewers defined it. Beer is meant to be fresh, exciting, varied, complex, flavorful, and alive. The homebrewing community resolved to bring delicious and interesting beer to the American market.

There have been plenty of hiccups and bad brews along the way to commercial craft-brewing success. Even highly popular offerings on the scene are not universally embraced. For every IPA-loving "hophead," there are probably a half-dozen beer drinkers who would like to see a wider array of Belgian- or German-style beers brewed in the United States. Although craft beer continues to claim a growing share of the market, beer drinking overall is down, as more imbibers turn to wine and artisanal spirits. But there's still plenty of room for growth and maturation in the American craft beer industry.

As a homebrewer, you're a member of this elite and dynamic group of beer revolutionaries. You have every chance of creating a new beer that will rock the craft beer world. You could harvest a new yeast strain or create a brand new beer style. There are no uncrossable boundaries. In this chapter, you'll learn how to trust your instincts and experiment with your own recipes. The ideas in this chapter are easy to put into action, now that you've learned to brew several different styles. Your solid beer knowledge will enable you to invent your own unique methods and brew your own unique beers.

BRAVE NEW BREWER

Hopefully by now, you're brewing beer you like to drink, and you've managed to create and replicate at least one great homebrew. If you've ventured onto the web in search of new beer recipes, you may have noticed that most of the online forums are pretty scant on details and probably offer ingredient lists, boil times, and not much more. When you first venture out to

brew, this recipe shorthand can be intimidating. However, now that you've brewed in a variety of styles, you're equipped to crack the home-brewing code. In fact, most homebrewers and professional brewers who post their recipes online fully expect you to make them your own.

The best way to create a new beer with an original twist is to make small changes to a recipe you've already mastered. It's easiest to learn the ins and outs of new recipe development by working with what you know before you start experimenting with unfamiliar ingredients and methods.

In addition to tweaking gravity (i.e., alcohol content), you can play with flavors. You may already have tried different hops in the IPA recipe in chapter 4. Learning the flavors of various hops and malts and figuring out what happens when you substitute others is very useful when you start making your own recipes from scratch. Try different yeast strains, as well. Do a *vertical tasting* of several beers in the same category to study the different qualities a beer style takes on with different ingredients.

Grow a garden. Fresh herbs and peppers, which you can easily raise in nearly any space, are great additions to beer. Find out what happens when you add jalapeños to the mix, tossing them in whole (with seeds) or seeded at various points in the brewing process. What happens when you dry hop with dandelion greens or change the boil times for certain ingredients?

On your expedition into new beer territory, your brewer's journal should be your constant companion. Take copious notes while you add various ingredients at different times during your boil, and during the early days of fermentation. Your journal is a record of what you did or should have done—invaluable information when you sample your new recipe a few weeks after going wild in the kitchen.

A MATTER OF TASTE

Another way to experiment with recipes is to put your brewmaking training to work. Now that you understand the mechanics of making a beer, you're ready to train your palate to understand what makes a beer taste great. Hopefully, you are now able to detect not just the aromas and flavors of various beers but the exact kinds of hops, malts, and yeast that make up those brews.

So, now it's time for some homework—the best homework you've ever been assigned. You'll have to wait at least two weeks before you get to sample your own beer, so you can spend that time getting acquainted with other beers, especially those made in the same style as the beer you just brewed or hope to brew soon. You'll also gain a more educated palate for detecting off-flavors in your own beer.

You may be thinking, "Wait a minute! How can I possibly compare my own beer with some of the best craft beer in America?" Why shouldn't you? The brewers at Sierra Nevada, Rogue, and Tröegs began their journeys the same way you have, by creating a batch of

PLAYING WITH GRAVITY

Start with something simple, like changing up the gravity. Changing your beer's gravity, thereby altering the ABV, is one of the easier ways to modify a beer, and you can do this in one of two ways:

- To raise gravity, add sugar to your wort: The addition of 1 pound of malt extract or corn sugar to a 5-gallon batch will raise the specific gravity by about 0.005. Adjust the sugar to make bigger or smaller changes in the gravity.

- To lower gravity, add water: The change you make in gravity by adding a given amount of water depends on the beer's original gravity. The heavier the OG, the greater the reduction in the specific gravity.

homebrew, tasting it, and learning to make better beer next time. If you continue to taste good beer, educate yourself, and adjust your brewing process, you will make better and better beer. In fact, the more beer you drink, the better you'll become at brewing your own.

This doesn't mean you should get drunk on a daily basis. Unlike wine drinkers, beer tasters don't typically spit out a beer unless it's rancid (an exception is sometimes made in judging). Tasting beer critically does take practice and a certain level of sobriety. In fact, the BJCP guidelines limit the number of beers a judge can sample during a single beer judging. You can't accurately judge a beer if you drink it while you're drunk, and you could end up wasting the best beer you've ever had. Training your palate is the time to "think while you drink."

LET'S GO CRAZY

Once you have a trained beer drinker's palate, you'll feel totally confident experimenting with what might well be considered "weird" ingredients. Honestly, the sky's the limit, but you might want to start with a few of the popular—albeit tricky—ingredients other brewers have successfully tried out. Some additions may set off your palate alarm, but experimentation is the name of the game when crafting new recipes.

COFFEE

When it comes to experimental brewing, nothing beats coffee. This is because there are so many different kinds of coffee to begin with. You could literally do nothing other than make coffee brews for the rest of your days. So begin with the obvious question: What kind of coffee do you want in your beer?

Obviously a stronger brew (e.g., espresso) will give you a more pronounced coffee flavor than a lighter coffee varietal (e.g., Guatemalan). In addition, you can add coffee to your beer in any of its forms: bean, ground, or brewed.

TO USE BREWED COFFEE Add 1 cup of coffee for every 2.5 gallons of wort either before you pitch your yeast or directly into the fermenter.

TO USE GROUND COFFEE Add ¼ cup ground coffee to your mash grains and mash per the regular recipe, draining out the grounds when you lauter.

TO USE WHOLE BEANS Add 1 cup of whole beans to your wort for the entire boil or 1 cup of crushed beans for 10 minutes at the end of the boil. (Note: You may want to use a grain bag to keep your coffee beans from getting stuck in the racking cane.)

You can also use cold-brewed coffee in making beer; simply add to your final fermentation before bottling or when adding sugars before kegging.

BREWING IDEAS Espresso stout, coffee (and) cream ale, coffee porter.

CHOCOLATE

As with hops and malt, there are many different forms in which you can add chocolate to beer. Among these: cocoa powder, cacao nibs, Baker's chocolate, chocolate extract, bar chocolate (typically, dark chocolate), or a combination of these. Chocolate has a lot of fatty properties, so you'll probably want to experiment with powder or roasted cacao nibs as opposed to melting a giant bar of chocolate into your boil.

The very best option for brewing with chocolate is unprocessed cocoa beans, which can be used exactly as you would coffee beans (either whole or ground). However, unprocessed beans are difficult to find, so try to use the least processed chocolate source available to you. This will probably be cocoa powder.

For a strong chocolate flavor, add the powder into your mash grains. For a less distinct chocolate flavor, you can sprinkle cocoa powder on top of the mash before sparging.

You can also experiment with chocolate extracts and liqueurs, adding them in before secondary fermentation or bottling. Try crème de cacao, for example, for a jolt of chocolate and alcohol in your beer.

Keep in mind that a little chocolate goes a long way, and many forms of malt already have chocolate notes in them.

BREWING IDEAS Chocolate porter, chocolate espresso stout, white chocolate pale ale.

BACON

There are two ingredients that don't generally work very well in brewing: protein and fat. Sadly, bacon is packed with both. However, thanks to many intrepid homebrewers like you, bacon beer is now a reality.

To make a beer with bacon in it, you will need approximately 1 ounce of cooked bacon per gallon of beer. Thus, 2.5 ounces for a yield of 24 12-ounce bottles. Begin by oven-cooking your bacon:

1. Line a cookie sheet with foil. If you like, place a metal cooling rack on the foil.

2. Lay raw bacon of average thickness on the foil or cooling rack.

3. Bake for 10 to 15 minutes at 400°F, making sure not to burn the bacon. The bacon should be thoroughly cooked until crisp.

4. Remove the bacon to cool on paper towels to absorb the extra fat.

When your wort is cooling in your carboy (or plastic bucket) and before you aerate or pitch your yeast, add bacon to your beer. Do not be surprised (or grossed out) if the bacon rehydrates and takes on a "raw" appearance. As the bacon cools, fat will congeal at the top of your carboy. You will need to rack your beer to the fermenter, keeping out the congealed fat (and bacon).

For a more pronounced bacon flavor, leave the cooked bacon in the fermenter for up to a week. Again, you will need to rack the beer into a fresh fermenter to get rid of the floating fat before completing fermentation. This technique is aptly called "fat washing" your beer.

BREWING IDEAS Smoked bacon rauchbier; "pig" porter; bacon chocolate stout.

NUTS AND SEEDS

Nuts and seeds make great additions to beer. Unlike bacon, the breadth of creativity in brewing with nuts is expansive. From almonds to coconut to peanut butter to walnuts to hazelnuts, you can go all nutty and come up with some amazingly nuanced brews. However, as with bacon, one of the chief challenges to adding nuts to your brew is to control for excess fat.

There are two main ways to brew with nuts or seeds: via roasting or via extract. To work with roasted nuts or seeds:

1. Spread unchopped nuts or whole seeds on a cookie sheet and bake at 350°F for 15 minutes.

2. Remove the nuts/seeds from the oven and spread them between paper towels to absorb the oil. Allow them to cool until they're safe to handle.

3. Chop the nuts/seeds finely and spread them out on a clean cookie sheet. Return them to the oven for another 15 minutes at 350°F.

4. Remove the pan from the oven and spread the nuts/seeds on paper towels to absorb the oil while cooling.

5. Put the nuts/seeds through steps 3 and 4 up to four times until toasted and thoroughly dried (i.e., no more oils are being released), using care not to burn them.

Some brewers like to leave the chopped nuts or seeds for a few days to get rid of the "roasted" taste; others like the additional flavor.

You can add your roasted nuts or seeds to the mash grains for steeping and strain out before the boil. Alternatively, you can steep them in hot water by themselves to make an extract. This "nut tea" should be put in the refrigerator, where the oils will congeal at the top of the extract. Remove all the congealed fat before you add the extract to the secondary fermenter before bottle conditioning. A secondary fermentation is the best way to incorporate a nut extract to your beer.

Keep in mind that some people have severe nut allergies, so clearly mark any beers that incorporate nuts or seeds.

BREWING IDEAS Pumpkin beer with pumpkin seeds; peanut butter stout; pistachio pale ale; sunflower seed saison.

OTHER IDEAS FOR CREATIVITY

Attempt to clone your favorite professionally brewed beer by selecting the ingredients you think will most closely match those in the brewer's recipe. You will want to be quite advanced in your tasting abilities (after you've successfully done *blind tastings*, for example). Otherwise, you can look at clone recipes on popular home-brew forums. You and your friends can then taste your clone and see how it compares to the original.

It's also exciting to try brewing historical beer styles. Beer historian Ron Pattinson, whose blog "Shut Up about Barclay Perkins" investigates phenomena such as lost beers, has researched many traditional styles that are rarely brewed anymore. You can find historical beer recipes in books (see Further Reading on page 85 for Pattinson's books) and online, but you can attempt to make an old-style beer even without a recipe. If you enjoy brewing a particular style of beer, look into its genealogy and try to work out a recipe that will reproduce the beer as it was first brewed.

Sometimes, you'll innovate out of necessity, such as to compensate for a missing ingredient. Other times, conceiving new beer recipes will be as much about developing beer you like to drink as experimenting just for the heck of it. Let your tastes and passion drive your creative process, and you may make some unique beers you'll want to share with your friends or other homebrewers.

FURTHER READING

GENERAL HOMEBREW AND CRAFT BEER "BIBLES"

Jackson, Michael. *The New World Guide to Beer.* Philadelphia, PA: Running Press, 1991.

Oliver, Garrett, ed. *The Oxford Companion to Beer.* New York, NY: Oxford University Press, 2012.

Papazian, Charlie. *The Complete Joy of Home Brewing.* 3rd ed. New York, NY: HarperCollins, 2003.

THE HISTORY OF HOMEBREWING IN AMERICA

Acitelli, Tom. *The Audacity of Hops: The History of America's Craft Beer Revolution.* Chicago, IL: Chicago Review Press, 2013.

Hindy, Steve. *The Craft Beer Revolution: How a Band of Microbrewers Is Transforming the World's Favorite Drink.* New York, NY: Palgrave MacMillan, 2014.

Ogle, Maureen. *Ambitious Brew: The Story of American Beer.* Orlando, FL: Harcourt, 2006.

THE SCIENCE OF HOMEBREWING

Bamforth, Charles. *Beer: Tap into the Art and Science of Brewing.* New York, NY: Oxford University Press, 2009.

Hieronymus, Stan. *For the Love of Hops: The Practical Guide to Aroma, Bitterness, and the Culture of Hops (Brewing Elements Series).* Boulder, CO: Brewers Publications, 2012.

Palmer, John, and Colin Kaminski. *Water: A Comprehensive Guide for Brewers (Brewing Elements Series).* Boulder, CO: Brewers Publications, 2013.

White, Chris, and Jamil Zainasheff. *Yeast: The Practical Guide to Beer Fermentation (Brewing Elements Series).* Boulder, CO: Brewers Publications, 2010.

CRAFT BEER STYLES AND TASTING TIPS

Bernstein, Joshua M. *The Complete Beer Course: Boot Camp for Beer Geeks: From Novice to Expert in Twelve Tasting Classes.* New York, NY: Sterling Epicure, 2013.

Brewers Association. "Brewers Association 2014 Beer Style Guidelines." Last modified March 10, 2014. Accessed September 9, 2014. www.brewersassociation.org/ educational-publications/beer-styles/.

Mosher, Randy. *Tasting Beer: An Insider's Guide to the World's Greatest Drink.* North Adams, MA: Storey Publishing, 2009.

RECIPE IDEAS

Fisher, Joe, and Dennis Fisher. *The Homebrewer's Garden: How to Easily Grow, Prepare, and Use Your Own Hops, Malts, Brewing Herbs.* North Adams, MA: Storey Publishing, 1998.

Koenig, Stephen, and Jamie Bogner, eds. *Craft Beer & Brewing 1*, no. 1 (Spring 2014).

Parks, Betsy, ed. *Brew Your Own: The How-To Homebrew Beer Magazine* 20, no. 2 (May/June 2014).

Pattinson, Ron. *The Home Brewer's Guide to Vintage Beer: Rediscovered Recipes for Classic Brews Dating from 1800 to 1965.* Minneapolis, MN: Quarry Books, 2014.

GLOSSARY

GENERAL

ALE: A beer fermented using top-fermenting yeast at a relatively high temperature (above 60°F) for a relatively short period of time (2–3 weeks).

CONTRACT BREWING: Brewing done at one brewery for another, known as the contract brewer. A contract brewer works either by renting space in another brewery and brewing there, or by paying another brewery to do all the work and then selling the beer under its own label.

CRAFT BEER: Beer brewed and marketed by relatively small, independent breweries. The precise definition most widely accepted by craft brewers is the one outlined by the Brewers Association (see page 35). The meaning of the term continues to evolve alongside the industry itself.

CRAFT BREWERY: An establishment that's in the business of making craft beer.

LAGER: A beer fermented using bottom-fermenting yeast at a relatively low temperature (45–55° F) for anywhere from four weeks to several months.

REINHEITSGEBOT: The German Beer Purity Law, dating to the 15th century, that restricts Bavarian brewers to only water, barley, hops, and yeast as ingredients in beer. Today, the law has been amended to permit the addition of certain sugars commonly used in beer making.

TRAPPIST: An official designation granted to beer brewed at Trappist monasteries following strict, traditional Trappist brewing practices. As of 2014, there were 11 working Trappist breweries in the world: 6 in Belgium, 2 in the Netherlands, 1 in Austria, 1 in Italy, and 1 in the United States.

INGREDIENTS

ADDITIVE: An ingredient added to wort to add flavor, such as fruits, spices, or additional sugars.

ADJUNCT: A non-malt–fermentable material (typically a grain) that provides sugars to feed yeast. Typical adjuncts include wheat, rye, rice, and corn.

ALL-EXTRACT: Describes beer made with liquid or powdered malt derived from grains.

ALL-GRAIN: Describes beer made without any malt extract.

ALPHA ACID: A chemical compound found in the resin glands of hop cones. Measured in Alpha Acid Units (AAU), it contributes to the bitterness of a brew. Hops are sold as varietals with specific alpha acid percentages that are indicated on the package labeling.

BARLEY: A cereal grain that, when malted, is the main ingredient in beer (after water).

BASE MALT: Also called "lager malt," this is the product of the first stage of malting, used in conjunction with other malts (kilned, roasted) to make different styles of beer.

BRETTANOMYCES: Typically referred to as "Brett," this wild yeast can appear naturally in beer or be intentionally added to lambic and other sour beers. This form of yeast can yield unpredictable results and challenges in fermentation.

CARAMELIZATION: The browning of sugars that takes place at high temperatures (230–356°F) during the malt-roasting process. It gives dark beer its typical flavors, such as toffee, molasses, and caramel.

CORN SUGAR: Dextrose that's typically added to beer just before bottling; promotes fermentation that carbonates the beer and raises its ABV.

CRYSTAL MALTS: Specialty grains that add flavor and color to beer; they can be mashed or steeped as a part of wort.

DEGREES LOVIBOND (°L): A measurement of color in malted grain.

DRY MALT EXTRACT (DME): Dry malt extract is produced by drying LME into crystalline form; used in place of mash.

HOPS: A flowering vine (*Humulus lupulus*) that produces cone-shaped flowers rich in resin and oils, giving beer its distinct bitter flavor and floral or fruity aroma.

LACTOBACILLUS: Lactic acid bacteria; it's often used in sour beer fermentation.

LIQUID MALT EXTRACT (LME): Liquid malt extract, derived from malted barley, is purchased premade and used in place of mash.

MALT: Grain that has been malted.

MALTED/MALTING: The process of activating the enzymes in a cereal grain to make its starches available for use (i.e., for mashing, in the case of brewing). Grain (typically barley) is softened in water and allowed to germinate, then heated and dried to halt germination. Malted grain is usually then toasted or roasted to varying degrees to bring out desirable colors and flavors.

MALTOSE: A sugar produced by the breakdown of starch in the malting process; a component of malt.

PEDIOCOCCUS: A lactic acid bacteria found in fermented foods and sour beers.

WILD YEAST: Yeast found in nature rather than cultivated in a laboratory. It can get into fermenting beer accidentally or be added intentionally to affect the flavors produced by fermentation.

YEAST: A microscopic fungus that digests sugars, causing fermentation that creates alcohol and carbon dioxide.

BREWING PROCESS

ALCOHOL BY VOLUME (ABV): The standard measure of how much alcohol is present in an alcoholic beverage.

ATTENUATION: The degree to which fermentation has converted sugars into alcohol and carbon dioxide, measured as a percentage.

BOIL: The process that creates wort by boiling water with malt derived from a mash or liquid extract.

BOTTLE BOMB: A bottle that blows its cap or explodes altogether during bottle conditioning. Fermentation after bottling can produce an excess of carbon dioxide, putting more pressure on the cap or glass than can be withstood.

BOTTLE CONDITIONING: The carbonation of bottled beer by ongoing fermentation; by contrast, kegged beer is carbonated by the addition of gas.

BOTTOM-FERMENTING: Describes yeast that settles to the bottom of the fermenter while producing alcohol; lagers are made with bottom-fermenting yeast.

BRIGHT WORT: The cleanest part of wort, generally recovered in the lautering process.

CHILL HAZE: Cloudiness in finished beer caused by the clumping of proteins in wort that's chilled too slowly after the boil.

COLD BREAK: The formation of proteins necessary for fermentation; occurs when wort is rapidly chilled after the boil.

DRY HOPPING: The process of adding hops directly to the fermenter (instead of during the boil); increases hop aroma without intensifying bitterness.

FINAL GRAVITY (FG): The density of a beer relative to that of water; one of the variables used to calculate ABV. See *gravity*.

FINING AGENT: A clarifying ingredient that's added to the boil to aggregate smaller molecules of extraneous matter into larger particles that will settle out of wort.

GRAVITY: The density of a liquid relative to that of pure water. Water has a gravity of 1.000; denser liquids (e.g., wort) measure >1.000 and lighter liquids (e.g., champagne) measure <1.000. The difference between original gravity and final gravity is used in calculating a beer's ABV. Gravity can be measured with a hydrometer. Most beers have a final gravity range between 1.014 and 1.005.

HOMEBREW COLOR UNITS (HCU): See *Standard Reference Method (SRM)*.

HOT BREAK: The rapid buildup of proteins in wort at the beginning of the boil, which causes the wort to foam up and potentially boil over.

INTERNATIONAL BITTERING UNIT (IBU): The measure of hop bitterness in a beer; notated from 0 (no hop presence) to 120+ (extreme hop presence).

LAGERING: Cold storage of beer during fermentation, typically used for beers containing bottom-fermenting yeast that prefers cooler temperatures. Lager beers are generally clear and clean tasting.

LAUTERING: A three-step, post-mash process that clears wort of residual grain matter while maximizing the retention of sugars and proteins in the wort.

MASH (N): A slurry of malted grains and the hot water in which they are steeped during mashing; mash is lautered to produce wort.

MASH (V): To steep malted grains in hot water to convert their starches into sugars and dissolve the sugars in the water. The process of mashing is usually called "the mash."

MASHOUT: The first step in lautering, in which the temperature of the mash is raised in order to stop further conversion of starches into sugars. Mashout also softens the sugars and keeps the grains from sticking together.

MILLING: The process of crushing malted grain to make its starches easier to convert to sugar during mashing.

ORIGINAL GRAVITY (OG): The density of wort compared to that of pure water; used to determine the concentration of malt sugar present. The most significant predictor of a finished beer's ABV.

PITCH: To add yeast to a fermenter.

RACK (V): To siphon wort from a fermenter while leaving behind the trub; wort can be racked either to secondary fermentation or straight into bottles.

RECIRCULATION: The second step in the lautering process, in which grain is strained out of the wort, which is then poured back over the grain into a clean brew pot. The process, which may be done several times depending on the wort, removes particulate matter and distributes proteins evenly throughout the wort.

SECONDARY FERMENTATION: An optional brewing technique, in which fermenting wort is siphoned off the trub into a second vessel for further fermentation and sometimes aging. The second vessel may be an ordinary fermenter, bottles, or an alternative container such as a wine or whiskey barrel.

SECONDARY WORT: Wort that's subject to secondary fermentation.

SPARGING: The third and final step in the lautering process, in which the last of the sugars are rinsed from the mashed grains into the wort. There are several sparging methods, including batch sparging, English sparging, and continuous sparging.

SPECIFIC GRAVITY: See *gravity*.

SPENT GRAIN: The mashed grain left over after lautering. Spent grain can be used in cooking, livestock feed, or compost.

STANDARD REFERENCE METHOD (SRM): A measure of beer color based on a range from 1 (very light) to 40+ (black); see also *degrees Lovibond (°L)*.

TOP-FERMENTING: Describes yeast that floats to the top of the fermenter while producing alcohol. Ales are generally made with top-fermenting yeast.

TRUB: The sediment produced during the hot break and cold break; it typically settles to the bottom of the fermenter and is carefully left behind during racking.

WET-HOPPING: The use of fresh hops in brewing.

WHIRLPOOLING: A method of separating trub and hops from wort after the boil. The wort is stirred to bring solids to the center of the brew pot, and the clear liquid is siphoned off from the sides.

WORT: A liquid made either by mashing (boiling) malted grain in water or mixing malt extract with water; the basis of beer.

EQUIPMENT

AIRLOCK: See "Equipment for Brewing (Required)" in chapter 3.

BLOWOFF HOSE: A length of food-grade plastic tubing inserted into the plug at the top of the fermenter to allow for the release of carbon dioxide. The hose directs the gas into a jar of water to bubble out. Serves the same purpose as an airlock; especially useful when vigorous fermentation might clog an airlock.

BOTTLE CAPPER: See "Equipment for Bottling (Required)" in Chapter 3.

BOTTLE FILLER: A rigid plastic or metal tube specifically made for filling bottles; usually it has a spring-loaded valve at the tip that allows you to start and stop the flow of beer by pressing the tip against the bottom of the bottle.

BOTTLING BUCKET: A food-grade plastic pail fitted with a spigot. You can attach tubing to the spigot for easy bottling. Using the spigot and tubing in place of a bottle filler allows you more control and makes it less likely you'll spill beer. This also eliminates the need for a siphon. Bottling buckets come in a variety of sizes.

BREW POT: See "Equipment for Brewing (Required)" in chapter 3.

CARBOY: A large (usually 5-gallon) plastic or glass bottle with a squat body and a short, narrow neck; used as a fermenter.

FERMENTER: See "Equipment for Brewing (Required)" in chapter 3.

FOOD-GRADE: Describes synthetic materials, such as plastics, that the US Food and Drug Administration has designated pure enough for food handling and storage.

HYDROMETER: See page 42.

KEGERATOR: A combination refrigerator/keg that's convenient for fermenting and tapping beer that isn't bottled.

LAUTER TUN: A pot-like vessel used to separate the liquid (wort) and solids (grains) of mash. Equipped with a slotted or perforated false bottom that holds the grains at the bottom of the pot, it has one or more drainage outlets that allow the wort to escape. A combination mash/lauter tun may be used instead.

MASH TUN: An insulated vessel, such as a cylindrical beverage cooler with a spigot, fitted with a false bottom (a screen that holds the grain in the bottom of the container). The insulation maintains the temperature of the mash during steeping. Similar to a lauter tun; can also be used for sparging.

SPECTROPHOTOMETER: An instrument that measures IBUs.

RACK/RACKING CANE: See "Equipment for Brewing (Required)" in chapter 3.

SANITIZER: See "Equipment for Brewing (Required)" in chapter 3.

SIPHON: See "Equipment for Bottling (Required)" in Chapter 3.

TUBING CLAMP: If you're using tubing to siphon your beer as you bottle, this will help control the flow so you don't spill beer.

WINE THIEF: A rigid 12- to 24-inch tube that assists in drawing samples of wort from the fermenter for testing without risking contamination of the whole batch. A sanitized turkey baster can serve the same purpose.

WORT CHILLER: A device used to chill wort quickly after the boil and cause a cold break. There are two main kinds: Immersion chillers pass cold water through a coiled tube immersed in hot wort; counter-flow chillers push hot wort through a coiled tube surrounded by cold water.

TASTING

ACETALDEHYDE: A chemical that causes an off-flavor of green apples; generally eliminated by aging the beer.

ACETIC: Describes a vinegary aroma most common in sour beers; caused by acetic acid bacteria.

ALDEHYDE: A chemical generated by the oxidation of alcohol; causes a variety of off-flavors, such as almond, or an aroma of perfume.

BEER JUDGE CERTIFICATION PROGRAM (BJCP): A training and certification program for beer judges, who must learn specific beer style guidelines.

BLIND TASTING: Evaluation of a beer without knowing what beer you're drinking.

DIACETYL: A strong off-flavor chemical typically compared with butter in both taste and aroma.

DIMETHYL SULFIDE (DMS): A strong off-flavor chemical typically compared with cooked corn in both taste and aroma.

ESTERS: Fruity aromas in ale.

HEAD RETENTION: Indicative of carbonation levels, with higher carbonation resulting in greater head retention—or how long the foam (i.e., head) lasts in a beer upon being served in a glass. Good head retention will remain to the last drop; average head retention will dissipate depending on how quickly the beer is finished or allowed to stand at room temperature; poor head retention is noted when the foam disappears after the beer is allowed to settle.

HORIZONTAL TASTING: Comparison of several beers across styles that share a similarity, such as flavor profile or ingredients.

MOUTHFEEL: The sensation of a beer's carbonation, body, and texture in the mouth.

OFF-FLAVOR: Any unintended or undesirable flavor that detracts from a beer's quality. Can be caused by poor sanitation, bacterial contamination, or various problems in the brewing or fermentation process.

PHENOLIC: A medicinal or industrial plastic smell related to off-flavors.

SESSIONABLE: Describes beers appropriate for drinking in quantity, owing to their low ABV.

SESSION BEER: A beer with a relatively low ABV, generally not exceeding 5.5%.

SKUNKED/SKUNKY: Describes a funky, sourish smell that can develop in beer that's overexposed to light. The aroma is often found in beers bottled in clear or green glass that doesn't filter out ultraviolet rays (brown glass filters them out).

VERTICAL TASTING: Comparison of several beers of the same style or an individual beer brewed on different dates.

INDEX

ABOUT THE AUTHOR

ASTRID COOK discovered craft beer whilst working on her first novel, and soon enough began writing about it. She is a member of Pink Boots Society and North American Guild of Beer Writers, where she has judged beer writing across the globe as part of their annual awards. Her work has appeared both online and in print at *All About Beer* Magazine, *West Coaster*, Complex.com and other beer-related websites.

ALSO IN THE DIY SERIES

Preserve nature's bounty and enjoy seasonal ingredients throughout the year.

Steep-by-steep (and step-by-step) recipes to create your own fresh, fragrant, and fizzy kombucha.

Enjoy homemade sauerkraut, kimchi, kombucha, kefir, yogurt, and other probiotic delights.

Unleash your inner kitchen crafter and master your pickling skills.

Harness the healing power of easy, affordable essential oils remedies.